ON GIDE'S *PROMÉTHÉE*

On Gide's
PROMÉTHÉE

PRIVATE MYTH AND PUBLIC MYSTIFICATION

BY KURT WEINBERG

Insipiens, tu quod seminas non vivificatur, nisi prius moriatur.—I COR. 15:36

PRINCETON UNIVERSITY PRESS · 1972

Publication of this book has been aided by
the Whitney Darrow Publication Reserve Fund
of Princeton University Press

Printed in the United States of America
by Princeton University Press,
Princeton, New Jersey

This book has been composed in Linotype Electra

Portions of the Introduction and of Chapter 1
appeared in German in *Der moderne französische
Roman: Interpretationen*, edited by
Walter Pabst (Berlin, 1968), pp. 77-102.
They are reprinted here by kind permission
of the publisher, Erich Schmidt Verlag.
A considerably shorter version of the remaining
chapters was published as "Doppelte Prädestination
und literarische Spiegeltechnik in André Gides
Le Prométhée mal enchaîné," in *Romanische
Forschungen*, LXXXI, no. 3 (1969).

For F.M.W. and O.G.B.

Contents

Preface

THE PRESENCE of a hermetic text exacts one of two attitudes: reverent silence, or the quest for a hermeneutics, permitting an exegesis. The critic who limits himself to the examination of the aesthetic structure helps to prolong silence, the *mutum* which is etymologically implied in *mysterium* and mystification. He sees in a book like Gide's *Le Prométhée mal enchaîné* little more than an expression of the artist's struggle with the elusiveness of his craft, a contrivance reflecting the polarity and the conflict of vital and artistic drives. He may become privy to the secrets of the master's workshop, and he may penetrate his techniques, his artistic scruples and agonies, as well as the mechanics of the work of art. But he fails to show aspects of the multivalent meaning, or to discover the temple hidden in the very forest of symbols, the spirit concealed in the letter. These can be approached only on the more perilous path of an interpretation founded upon the rigorous discipline of hermeneutics. This path will be followed in my analysis. The Introduction constitutes an effort to abstract from a cursory glance at the novel (since Rousseau), and from Gide's literary theory, hermeneutical principles which could serve as a basis for an interpretation of the *Prométhée*. The remainder of this essay is devoted to such an exegesis.

The quest for a literary hermeneutics has its dangers. Each author, each book requires an individual approach. Typological interpretation cannot become a matter of routine. The methodological search for an exegetic avenue to the *Prométhée* reaches into Gide's idiosyncrasies, into his changing attitudes which leave intact the dichotomy of his Arcadian libertinage and his obsessive Calvinism. It places the *Prométhée* within the context of Gide's total work, the fictional discovery of *la vie en puissance*; of Gide's life not as it was but as it could have been, as fantasies transposed into fiction. Gide's sinuous *sotie à tiroirs* calls not for a rectilinear but a spiraling exploration. It is at heart a *sotie à miroirs*, episodical, each episode mirroring all other episodes, the first one containing the whole "plot," every subsequent one varying and slightly distorting the previous ones. My definition of Kafka's novelistic structure also holds for the *Prométhée*: the infinitely reflected series of repetitions takes the place occupied in the traditional novel by the progression of action.[1] The apparent circularity of my examination of tropes and topics, which *in specula speculorum* reflects my speculations, does not extend to the movement of my argumentation. It may nonetheless be a source of irritation to the reader. But in the end he will realize that it systematically links the aesthetic structure and moral intentions of the *sotie* with Gide's intimate world of private associations, revealing the devious meaning of a grotesque and all but gratuitous humor which has puzzled generations of critics and biographers alike.

My interpretation, of course, involves a gamble where the risks may seem to outweigh the gains; and my impetuous commitment to *serio ludere*, no doubt, will appear ludicrous to the positivist scholar. But it is in keeping with the spirit of Gide's *sotie*, and is likely to shed some light on a text which might otherwise prove unintelligible.

The original edition of the *Prométhée* (1899), which I was unable to consult before the completion of this study, is followed by thirty-three *Réflexions*, which have been omit-

---

[1] Kurt Weinberg, *Kafkas Dichtungen: Die Travestien des Mythos* (Bern and Munich: Francke Verlag, 1963), p. 85.

ted since the 1920s when the *Nouvelle Revue française* re-issued the book, for, by then, they had appeared in Gide's *Journaux* (and elsewhere). A number of these aphorisms coincide with those which, independently, I had selected from the *Journaux* in support of my interpretation. I am tempted to believe that this coincidence, more than any reasoned argument, helps to cement my thesis: the *Prométhée* reflects the ironic dichotomy between Gide's aesthetic pursuit of purity (in literature) and his amoral ethos (in life). While Gide the amoralist aims at discrediting Calvinist Puritanism, Gide the author taps and exploits it as the main source of his fiction.

Finally, I wish to express my profound gratitude to my distinguished colleagues and friends Peter Dunn, the Hispanist, Eléonore M. Zimmermann, the comparatist, John H. Wright, the classicist, as well as to Joanna Hitchcock, my most stimulating manuscript editor, for the care and patience with which they have read my typescript.

Brighton, New York
May 1971

Abbreviations

ARABIC numerals in parentheses refer to page numbers in André Gide, *Romans, récits et soties, œuvres lyriques* (Paris: Nouvelle Revue française, Bibliothèque de la Pléiade, 1958).

J. 1	*Journal 1889-1939* (Paris: Nouvelle Revue française, Bibliothèque de la Pléiade, 1951).
J.d.F.-M.	*Journal des Faux-Monnayeurs* (Paris: Nouvelle Revue française, 1948).
M.ch.	*Morceaux choisis* (Paris: Nouvelle Revue française, 1935).
Inc.	*Incidences* (Paris: Nouvelle Revue française, 1948).
Corr.F.J.-A.G.	*Correspondance d'André Gide avec Francis Jammes* (Paris: Gallimard, 1948).
Dostoïevsky	*Dostoïevsky: Articles et causeries* (Paris: Plon, 1923).
Litt.eng.	*Littérature engagée* (Paris: Nouvelles Revue française, 1950).
Institutio	Jean Calvin, *Christianae religionis Institutio* (Basel, 1536).

ON GIDE'S *PROMÉTHÉE*

Este buitre voraz de ceño torvo
que me devora las entrañas fiero
y es mi único constante compañero
labra mis penas con su pico corvo.

El día en que le toque el postrer sorbo
apurar de mi negra sangre, quiero
que me dejéis con él solo y señero
un momento, sin nadie como estorbo.

Pues quiero, triunfo haciendo mi agonía,
mientras él mi ultimo despojo traga,
sorprender en sus ojos la sombría

mirada al ver la suerte que le amaga
sin esta presa en que satisfacía
al hambre atroz que nunca se le apaga.

Unamuno, *Rosario de Sonetos líricos*

Dagegen hat der Liebhaber, Kenner, Ausleger
völlig freie Hand, die Symbole zu entdecken,
die der Künstler bewusst oder bewusstlos in
seine Werke niedergelegt hat.

(However, the connoisseur, the exegete, is totally free to discover the symbols which the
artist has consciously or unconsciously de-
posited in his work.—Goethe to S. Boisserée,
July 16, 1818.)

Introduction GIDE AND THE NOVEL

1. The Confessional Novel and Narcissism

"A NOVEL [*Roman*] is a romantic book," declares Antonio, somewhat perplexingly, in Friedrich Schlegel's *Gespräch über die Poesie* (1800). His formula would seem tautological, were it not for the Schlegels' broad definition of "romantic": as universal poetry the novel is meant to embrace the grotesque, the lyric, the epic, drama, myth, irony. It holds a mirror to history (contemporary and past) but, above all, it provides veiled insights into the author's intimate world. The novel, a poetic mixture of genres in prose (*Mischgedicht*), simultaneously allows the epic display of actions, the dramatic vivisection of passions and delusions, the lyrical gamut of egotistical self-contemplation, and the grotesque spectacle of avowed (if highly questionable) public confession: "the best in the best novels is but the author's more or less concealed personal confession, the result of his experience, the quintessence of his idiosyncrasy" (*ibid.*). In contrast to the Stoic (or classical) concept of the world as a stage where every actor must play a preordained role, incarnate a character unchangeable and predestined by fate, the Christian doctrine of man's freedom of will permits unforeseeable choices and changes in character. This freedom survives in the largely post-Christian lay culture of Gide's age, where it mingles with motley fragments of devaluated Christianity (which later will be reborn) and with Hegelian and post-Hegelian determinism. It manifests itself in a disparate search for idiosyncrasies which the novelist may observe in himself, analyze, graft onto, and satirize in his fictional heroes (and

3

antiheroes). It is a form of narcissism where self-love more often than not turns into dramatic self-hatred, but in the end, by way of revolt against excessive guilt feelings, changes back with a vengeance to its original nature (if not to its primal, unreflective innocence). Self-analysis as a public posture—under the veil of fiction and in the form of aggressive self-adulation, self-flagellation, or a combination of both attitudes—is a way of life (and, as fiction, a surrogate for life) in the Christian and post-Christian world.

There is, however, nothing new about self-analysis in literature. Augustine practiced it with the savoir faire of the sophistically trained master of rhetoric. His *Confessions* aim to persuade, to convert. Montaigne, with the amused detachment of the *grand seigneur*, tried to discover a constant beneath the passing flow of his sensations, insights, emotional and intellectual reactions. But there is something new and theatrical about the Calvinist discipline of public confession as it enters French literature with Rousseau, in whom Nietzsche recognizes the first modern man: half idealist, half *canaille*. With Rousseau, self-analysis turns into self-gratification: a type of narcissism which runs the full gamut from self-attraction to self-accusation, from self-pity to self-mortification. The resources of rhetoric—figures of speech and topoi, commonplaces—are used to persuade us not of literary verisimilitude but of the author's personal "sincerity." *Ecce homo* becomes the persuasive posture for a new kind of *captatio benevolentiae*: the novelist, crucified by his enemies, sentimentally or ironically superimposes his image upon that of his heroes. He blackens himself so as to appear more human than his opponents; and since he frankly admits weaknesses and sins, he looks more virtuous than those who are said to be his relentless persecutors. Valéry once suggested that "he who confesses, lies," thus echoing the ambiguous title of Goethe's autobiographical *Dichtung und Wahrheit* ("Fiction and Truth") and Heine's warning to the readers of his own "confessions" (*Geständnisse*). From confessional literature issued a fictional hero who, in many variations, proliferates throughout Romantic literature: a lonely exile in the crowd, estranged, narcissistic, suffering from incestuous drives, masochistic obsessions, or sexual impotence, haunted by guilt and often seeking in death the fulfillment of his forbidden loves. Stripped of his guilt complex, sentimentality, perversions, impotence, and death wishes, and justified as a stranger in a world whose morality he rejects, he can still be recognized in Camus's Meursault. Rousseau's dramatic self-display (not as he was, but as he carefully made himself up for a public performance) may be described as a relatively uninhibited type of narcissism. It first appears in *La Nouvelle Héloïse* (1756-1761), comes to its flowering in the three dialogues, *Rousseau juge de Jean-Jacques* (1772-1776), and reaches its maturity in *Les Confessions*. Since the author cannot intervene in the body of an epistolary novel, Rousseau uses footnotes in *La Nouvelle Héloïse* to correct and annotate the opinions of his characters, while two prefaces explain why Rousseau, the avowed foe of fiction, uses fiction of all things to combat the "nefarious effects" of that very form on the "corrupt Society" of his age. With Saint-Preux, Rousseau sets a precedent for a large number of future novelists whose heroes and antiheroes will reflect an idealized image of the author: as Satanic protagonists, savior figures, or diabolical redeemers, they will be shown in the process of watching themselves act out their lives, while their author, in autobiographic confessions, memoirs, diaries, and dialogues, corrects their fortunes *post facto*. In short, literary narcissism determined some of the major themes, most of the fictional characters, and even the lyrical overtones of the French novel from Senancour and Chateaubriand to Gide, Malraux, and Camus.

A common belief in the ability to communicate human experience (shown as it is or as it ought to be) linked the novelists of the seventeenth and eighteenth centuries to their successors in the nineteenth, regardless of whether they were *moralistes* or moralizers. They could all have subscribed to Stendhal's idea of the novel as a mirror held up to the life-long comedy of the human heart: to folly, delusions, self-deception—for Stendhal, the necessary ingredients of happiness, and for Flaubert, the scorned elements of *bovarysme*. The mirror of the novel was meant to reflect the protagonist's subjective impressions in objective images which touched a sympathetic cord in the reader's heart because of a sensibility he shared with the author. "A novel is like the bow of a violin; the sounding board which gives forth the sound is the reader's soul," Stendhal could still say in the 1840s. Stendhal could think of his own perspectivist[1] egotism (and of that of his heroes) as universally intelligible; and of his theory of crystallization as generally true for a sort of human folly which accompanies love, "reflecting all perfections and turning into perfection everything in the object which leaves its imprint on the matrix." Stendhal trusts in experiences common to all humans of a certain level of intelligence or sensi-

---

[1] *Das Perspektivische, perspektivisch, Perspektivismus* are epistemological terms used by Nietzsche to stress that all cognition is relative to "perspective," i.e., the vital needs and biases of the person who ascertains knowledge: "seeing exists *only* as seeing under a given perspective (*perspektivisches Sehen*), knowledge *only* as knowledge under a given perspective (*perspektivisches Erkennen*). (*Zur Genealogie der Moral,* aphorism 12, in *Werke,* ed. Karl Schlechta [Munich, 1955] II, 861.) From Nietzsche's usage, the French have derived the noun *perspectivisme.* Since there is no corresponding term in the English language, I have coined the adjective "perspectivist(ic)" in order to characterize a phenomenon in the modern novel which enables the reader to see fictional reality as it becomes multiply diffused through the individual "perspectives" of a number of characters, or through the schizophrenic vision of one and the same protagonist.

bility as the key to the understanding of these phenomena. "The happy few" to whom he addresses his books and the reader of 1890 (or perhaps 1930) will understand the peculiarities of his egotism, which compels him to show a particular individual's emotional reactions rather than to describe factual situations, both in his fictional characters and his autobiographical writings. His future reader will easily recognize the author's intention not to depict things, but the impact of things upon a special egotistic sensitivity.

The Romantic illusion of "realism" in the visionary configurations of Balzac, Flaubert, and even Zola remained possible as long as the novel was considered to be a work of art which truthfully mirrors mores and characters, while transforming bourgeois mediocrity and proletarian drabness into beauty through the purifying alchemy of style. It remained possible so long as one could agree with Stendhal's definition of character as a person's customary way of pursuing happiness, and accept as the sum total of a character's moral habits the particular form which this hedonistic quest might take. This formula fits French eighteenth-century fiction as well. Since the time of Prévost, the novel had continued the function which in the seventeenth century, according to Boileau, had fallen to French classical comedy: "Chacun peint avec art dans ce nouveau miroir."[2] For, in spite of their picaresque

[2] *Art poétique*, III, 353. The eighteenth-century *romancier-moraliste* wanted to establish his role as a *moraliseur*. Cf. even Rousseau's "Seconde Préface de la nouvelle Héloïse," and, more strikingly, de Laclos's "Préface du rédacteur" of *Les Liaisons Dangereuses*: "Il me semble au moins que c'est rendre un service aux moeurs, que de dévoiler les moyens qu'emploient ceux qui en ont de bonnes, et je crois que ces lettres pourront concourir efficacement à ce but. On y trouvera aussi la preuve et l'exemple de deux vérités importantes qu'on pourrait croire méconnues, en voyant combien peu elles sont pratiquées: l'une que toute femme qui consent à recevoir dans sa société un homme sans moeurs, finit par en devenir la victime; l'autre, que toute mère est au moins

realism, seventeenth-century novels thematically as wide apart as Sorel's satirical *Histoire comique de Francion* and Scarron's thespian *Le Roman comique* had remained episodic narratives of adventures in travel and sex. In their own quite different ways they were as close to the formal tradition of Heliodoros's *Ethiopian History* as was Mlle Scudéry's *Le Grand Cyrus*. With *La Princesse de Clèves*, the novel had gained psychological depths equaling (without outdistancing) Corneille's and Racine's explorations of conflicts between will and passion. It had indeed made great strides as a mirror of manners in the fictions of Duclos, Crébillon, Nerciat, and Restif de la Bretonne. *La Nouvelle Héloïse*, which contrasted middle-class concepts of virtue, comfort, and the idyllic life with aristocratic libertinage, good breeding (*les bienséances*), and (generally uncomfortable) grandeur, while exalting manners as they ought to be rather than depicting them as they are—a novel devoid of the most elementary psychology, reflecting and condensing for the French reader the Swiss ideals of Muralt, Haller, and Bodmer—had become the moral, political, and sentimental book of commonplaces for personalities as varied as Marie-Antoinette, Saint-Just and Robespierre, Marat, Bernardin de Saint-Pierre, and Sade. "Que de vigueur, que d'énergie dans l'Héloïse; . . . l'amour lui-même traçait de son flambeau toutes les pages brûlantes de Julie, et l'on peut dire avec raison que ce livre sublime n'aura jamais d'imitateurs," raves the Marquis de Sade in his *Idée sur les romans*, pretending to show the corruption of society under the monarchy, while indulging in unbridled anal fantasies of sex, violence, and murder, the monotony of which is broken in

---

imprudente, qui souffre qu'une autre qu'elle ait la confiance de sa fille. Les jeunes gens de l'un et de l'autre sexe, pourraient encore y apprendre que l'amitié que les personnes de mauvaises moeurs paraissent leur accorder si facilement n'est jamais qu'un piège dangereux, et aussi fatal à leur bonheur qu'à leur vertu . . ." (Brussels, 1885, pp. x-xi).

his novels and plays by passionately rational discourses on the natural right of the individual to erect his orgiastic freedom upon the total sacrifice of his victims. Sade's libertines, unredeemably imprisoned in the infernal circle of their vices, their criminal imagination and insatiable appetites, evoke the universe of a concentration camp, an inferno of crapulence and absurdity such as one finds portrayed with equal vigor and frankness in Jean Genet's *Journal d'un voleur* and *Notre-Dame-des-Fleurs*. From *La Nouvelle Héloïse* Stendhal had learned the difference between what he called *l'esprit appris* (the conventions of Parisian polite conversation) and *l'esprit spontané* (Octave's sound, original, and spontaneous insights in *Armance*). On the other hand, Stendhal's portrayal of Octave's attractive misanthropy can be traced to Rousseau's treatment of Molière's Alceste (*Le Misanthrope*) in *Lettre à d'Alembert, sur les spectacles*. Hidden in ambiguously ironic fiction and determining the lives, for example, of Julien Sorel, Mme de Rênal, and even Emma Bovary, we find the gamut of Rousseauist commonplaces: unfulfilled fantasies, bourgeois prudishness, the blundering good faith of rustic characters, and the innate nobility of energetic autodidacts who rise from the lower classes, their corruption by urbane ambitions and courtly society, by the Church and immoral (if inane) novels, and their possible (but not necessary) redemption after their "fall" and subsequent return to simplicity.

It was Rimbaud and Mallarmé, not novelists but poets, who were among the first to challenge the traditional faith in communication, and to question the naïve trust placed by the Naturalists in positivism, in scientific observation, in an objective reality which was supposed to remain intact even when perceived *à travers un tempérament*, a physiological constitution (as suggested by Zola in *Le Roman expérimental*). It is significant that Gide as well as Valéry, Claudel, and other prominent figures made their literary debuts in Mallarmé's *salon*. The supposedly objective mirror of the novel shattered upon contact with the esoteric of Symbolism, just as the indivisibility of the individual had been fatally affected by the Cartesian dualism of body and soul. Simultaneously, the very foundation of the novel of the individual—the art of literary portraits and character sketches inherited from the seventeenth century—breaks into a thousand splinters which mirror the fragmentary reflections of an irretrievably lost unity.

With the collapse of the belief in an objective reality—intelligible to the reader as perceived and proposed to him by the novelist—there also vanishes that faith in the irrefutability of the "document" (so meticulously used by a skeptic like Flaubert) and the reliance on unequivocal "facts," "scientifically" established situations, social and medical data (still trusted by Zola). What remains is the schizophrenic vision of the neurotic protagonist, a world without claims to objectivity, universality and intelligibility, where fantasies are inextricably intermingled with uncertain flashes emanating from external reality. This intimate vision, seen through the eyes of one or several characters, finds expression in the novel, without being fully communicable. The reader embarks with Proust on a voyage that leads through fleeting remembrances to the final recovery of time "lost," yet preserved in the subconscious depths of memory: the special world of Swann and Marcel blends without fixed chronology into a specific period of French history. The reader ventures into the hero's personal maze of symbols to discover in the end the thread of Ariadne that guides him out into the open whence, at last, he can gain a perspective on the whole. The way is prepared for *Finnegans Wake* and for the paranoid and schizophrenic *nouveau roman* with its multilevel structure and Gothic humor. The author may still intervene in his work, but he may no longer interpret his characters. The fictitious events, nonevents, and "happenings" may have a logic of their own, immanent in the protagonist's split personality, in his amnesia, in his inability to grasp the forces that link him to the past and the present; yet there seems to exist no rational clue to the sequence of repetitive scenes and images. They remain unintelligible, fragmented, obsessively recurrent even in the dim and confused rationalizations which the protagonist may apply to the often insoluble puzzle of his trivial, drab, unexciting fate. The author and his protagonist have at their disposal symbols and archetypes common to both; but all commonplaces which had formerly established a bond between novelist and reader seem to be lost. No topoi, no universal categories of reason appear to offer clues to the protagonist's behavior, to his broken vision of the world around him which seems to offer him no refuge: only his gestures, meaningless tokens of his disorientation, are recorded as ostensibly disconnected phenomena.

Long before the contemporary novel began to explore the grotesque and violent wasteland of the absurd and the morphology of tropisms,[3] Gide substituted for the commonplaces and traditional logic of fiction "un monde spécial dont [l'artiste a] seul la clef" (*J.* I, 94). What had been the domain of vanguard poetry and fiction since Baudelaire, Rimbaud, Flaubert, Huysmans, Villiers de l'Isle-Adam, and Barbey d'Aurevilly is now found wanting: the exaltation of artifice over nature, "decadence" (at the end of the second Christian millennium), the artist's awareness of man's accelerated and irredeemable fall. The mere discovery of perverse sensations and new artistic devices leaves the Gide of 1894 unsatisfied. To satisfy his artistic conscience, they must pass through the diffuse filter of a "strongly coloured idiosyncrasy" (*ibid.*). In short, the *roman à clef* must be converted into

[3] Cf. Nathalie Sarraute, *Tropismes* (Paris, 1957).

an idiosyncratically ciphered *mythe à clef*, a private myth to which the reader may only gain access if as an "initiate"—in the language of the Symbolists—he can find clues to the novelist's intimate world of references: to his private associations, parables, truths. "Le symbole, c'est autour de quoi se compose un livre," hints Gide, and in another aphorism: "... l'oeuvre d'art, c'est une idée qu'on exagère" (*ibid.*). This type of oracular wisdom conforms both to Gide's irony and to the spirit of the times. It faintly echoes the Pre-Raphaelites, the marriage of decadence and perverted, anemic childlikeness in *fin de siècle* art and literature, the artificial fairytale world of Maeterlinck's plays (greatly admired by the young Gide), the esoterics, musicality, and suggestiveness in the works of Mallarmé, his disciples, and their allies. More clearly it points back to the *Notebooks* and *Poetry* of André Walter, Gide's first (still unsigned) publications which are imbued with reminiscences of readings in early nineteenth-century German poets whose metric rhythms (alien to French syllabic verse) the youthful Gide had sought to capture. Gide's aphorisms recall Novalis, the Schlegels, and Goethe, for whom the novel "presents possible events, under both possible and impossible conditions, still as possible events" (*Maximen und Reflexionen*, no. 1047). Gide's early concept of "symbol" may well derive in part from Goethe's definitions: "In true Symbolism the particular represents the universal, not as dream or shadow but as a living and instantaneous revelation of the inscrutable" (*ibid.*, no. 314); "Symbolism transforms the phenomenon into an idea, the idea into an image, so that the idea remains forever infinitely effective and inaccessible in the image, and unspeakable even if expressed in all languages" (*ibid.*, no. 1113). By contrast "allegory transforms the phenomenon into a concept, the concept into an image—the concept being completely contained, beheld, and expressed in the image" (*ibid.*, no. 1112).

In this sense "allegories" allow of only one narrowly limited, conceptual interpretation, whereas "symbols" are open to numerous exegeses, all equally valid as long as they express the same universal truth which is alive and accessible in the thoughtful presentation and description of the symbol itself. When the novelist refines his art, as does the young Gide, to the point where he metamorphoses his personal world of symbols into coded allegories and personally transforms Hellenic, Hellenistic, and Christian myths, then he prepares the way for the first Surrealist manifesto, where the pseudo-Voltairean fiction of Anatole France is buried three decades later, together with its author, under the heading "Un Cadavre."

In the 1890s, when he was both imitating and parodying Symbolism, Gide's literary experimentation with myth was more daring than that of his later ventures. From Rousseau he had learned the art of self-concealment behind the façade of public confessions, but narcissism in his early fiction noticeably suffers from inhibitions which betoken its loss of innocence. Gide's searching and ironic early productions gave birth to a type of critical self-consciousness which adds a new dimension to fiction: now the writer qua writer invades the novel in the guise of a fictional novelist or in person, introducing discussions on the theory of the novel. The brutal reality of criticism, bursting into the world of fiction, threatens to cancel out the poetic illusion, substituting, as it were, nature for art. In a medium that is meant to convey mythical truth through the behavior of fictional characters, the reader is unexpectedly faced with the author's personal truth: his frustrations in his search for new forms of narrative and his struggle with fabulation amid the elusiveness of reality and protagonists. For inner and outer "reality" alike, seen in the mirror of the protagonists' purely subjective rationalizations, seem to be abolished in the very confusion of contradictory aspects.

Like Rousseau, Gide extended his novels beyond their covers, commenting on his completed fictions in essays and in a diary, literally written before the mirror, and periodically published for the benefit of his reading public. Criticism, confessional fiction, and fictional confessions supplement each other, attacking the form of the novel at its very foundation, and affecting it by the expression of doubt in the possibility of mimetic art. For Gide is skeptical of "imitations" of a "reality" which can only be perceived through the splintered mirror of the protagonist's subjective imagination: fragmentary, reflected, perspectivistic. The narrator's intellectual and psychological integrity becomes doubtful; and the *raison d'être* of the genre and its "purity" become obsessive to an author whose "purism" seems to be largely symptomatic of his lifelong struggle with a Puritanism of which he cannot rid himself. The novel serves Gide in two extrafictional ways: by disseminating his disquieting, immoralist ethos, and by providing him with a platform from which he can theorize *ex cathedra* on the formal purity that he tries to impose on a genre doomed to impurity, whose form is bound to be marred by the inevitability of hackneyed phrases and the trivialities of everyday occurrences. For the novelist encounters his moment of truth when, like Proust, he has to say what Valéry could never bring himself to write: "La marquise sortit à cinq heures." We have seen that, by discussing problems of fiction within the fiction itself, Gide carried the novel beyond its confines. When the novelist's aesthetic and moral attitudes, his conflict between artistic creation and life, are encompassed by the very tensions of the novel, then literary narcissism reaches phenomenological proportions: the protean phenomenon "novel" is now captured by phenomenology. Juxtaposed to the action and intermingling with it, the work of art becomes its own object, pleading within its own pages for its very right to exist. Directly

or by implication, the writer's study appears on the scene i_
all of Gide's early works (in the *Prométhée* it is briefly
glimpsed before the Epilogue). It is the alchemist's labora-
tory where the magnum opus of purification is supposed to
operate upon the genre.

In a variety of approaches, Wolfgang Kayser, Harry Levin,
and Georges May[4] have diagnosed the perennial crisis of the
novel, which seems to have afflicted it since its beginnings.
It reaches proportions beyond control once the novelist trans-
gresses into his fiction, no longer as a commentator on mores,
environment and behavior, but (like Gide) in order to play
the theorist, aesthetician, and critic of the novel, defining
the genre in its "purity" and distinguishing it from the more
"impure" forms of other types of fictional discourse and narrative. The ever-repeated experiment to produce the "pure"
novel must fail again and again, since the novelist (in his own
words) must refuse to benefit from his *élan*, from the mo-
mentum gained in the process of writing. Every step, every
chapter must be the result of a new start: a new impetus
(*J.d.F.-M.*, 28, 77, 93), already given to a fictional character
in the *Prométhée*[5] (326), will be applied in similar fashion
almost thirty years later in *Les Faux-Monnayeurs*.

In his early works (e.g., *Paludes*), as well as in the *Journal
des Faux-Monnayeurs*, Gide casts suspicions on undertakings
of this nature. Even if they are attempted by deceptively

[4] Wolfgang Kayser, *Entstehung und Krise des modernen Romans*,
2nd ed. (Stuttgart, 1955); offprint, DVIG, xxviii, no. 4; Georges May,
Le Dilemme du roman au XVIIIe siècle (New Haven and Paris, 1963);
Harry Levin, *The Gates of Horn: A Study of Five French Realists*
(New York, 1966).

A comprehensive study of the lyrical qualities of the Romantic and
post-Romantic novel was successfully carried out by Ralph Freedman,
*The Lyrical Novel: Studies in Hermann Hesse, André Gide, and Vir-
ginia Woolf* (Princeton, 1963).

[5] *Prométhée* refers to *Le Prométhée mal enchaîné*, Prometheus to
the hero of the *sotie*.

autobiographic projections of himself (such as Édouard in *Les Faux-Monnayeurs*), they suggest the intellectual and emotional sleight of hand, the counterfeit work of art. Gide's didactic novels are towers of Babel where each protagonist speaks an incommunicable language of his own which leads him astray into the false paradise of self-deception. They are labyrinths where the reader perceives through the eyes of the protagonists contradictory perspectives which are constantly in danger of canceling each other out, although sometimes (especially in *La Porte étroite* and *La Symphonie pastorale*) dramatic irony allows the reader to see distinctly the subtle devices of a peculiar type of hubris, well known to Gide from experience: the blinding results of Calvinist self-righteousness. Gide's fictional novelists suffer from the same puritanical weakness, aesthetically sublimated. Their quest for the grail is a quest for a personal "purity" and "authenticity" which, they expect, will produce in mysterious ways the "purification" of their *œuvre*. There is a goodly portion of Rousseauist naïveté involved in this view of a causal relationship between the author's personal purity, sincerity, and authenticity and the appearance, the illusion of these qualities in his fiction which, after all, must be the effect of his art and not of his nature. But even where the artist's nature is concerned, his enterprise is doomed to failure, for his person is *persona*, "impure," "unauthentic." Despite its mobility, it is but the rigid mask of his existence as social conventions and early traumata have fashioned it: a protean phenomenon of mimicry and hypocrisy, variable in its illusory being and never fully intelligible even to its owner. In the end, the attempt to strive for purity, authenticity, amoral and immoral freedom is unmasked as a temptation, a deception and self-deception, a pathetic disillusionment which destroys heroes as different as Gide's Narcisse, Lafcadio, and the minister of

La Symphonie pastorale, but also the prodigal son, a rebel too weak for rebellion, whose return marks his failure.

Gide's fictional writers are equally quixotic, pursuing the phantom of the "pure novel" only to experience at the end of their impossible quest an overpowering realization of failure, a feeling of sterility. "Purger le roman de tous les éléments qui n'appartiennent pas spécifiquement au roman" is the goal that Édouard, the writer-hero of *Les Faux-Monnayeurs,* has set for himself. But like Tityre, his predecessor in *Paludes* thirty years earlier, he is not permitted to attain his goal. Nevertheless, like Sisyphus he must perpetually repeat his hopeless labors, even though like Camus's Sisyphus he is allowed to enjoy the dignity of reflecting upon his lot during his way downwards: "ce pur roman, il ne parviendra jamais à l'écrire" (*J.d.F.-M.,* 62ff., 65). (Gide has the sudden revelation of his lifelong attempts to write "pure" novels after his encounter with the concept of "pure poetry," formulated by the Abbé Bremond in 1925: it is clearly a retroactive transfiguration of the past as the result of a formula suddenly revealed to him.)[6]

To Gide's vain quest for the "pure" novel corresponds his hesitation to name his works of fiction "novels." Only *Les Faux-Monnayeurs* benefits from this designation. Provisionally he may call his narrative works "novels"; ultimately however they are grouped as *récits* ("narratives") and *soties* (a type of allegorical farce which will be defined below). The *Prométhée,* originally called a "novel," was reclassified as a *sotie* fifteen years later, when Gide published another *sotie, Les Caves du Vatican.* In 1914, Gide somewhat mysteriously contrasted his *récits* and *soties* with the novel; he did not qualify his statement, establishing these distinctions between

[6] Cf. H. Bergson, *La Pensée et le mouvant,* 22nd ed. (Paris, 1946), p. 16.

different forms of fiction without explaining how he wanted them to be understood: "Pourquoi j'appelle ce livre [Les Caves du Vatican] *sotie?* Pourquoi *récits* les trois précédents? Pour bien marquer que ce ne sont point là des *romans* (*J.* I, 437); July 12, 1914).

2. *The* Prométhée: *A Structural Anticipation of* Les Faux-Monnayeurs

Considering the brevity of the *Prométhée*, its architecture is remarkably complex. Here the multilevel structure of the *roman à tiroirs,* analogous to that of the *Arabian Nights,* reaches extreme proportions. It would seem as though the episodic novel, by nature a grotesque and burlesque genre, parodied itself in the *Prométhée.* In this display of formal virtuosity and narcissistic self-reflection, the *Prométhée* already exhibits that type of *serio ludere* which, twenty-five years later, was to characterize *Les Faux-Monnayeurs.* More surprisingly still, the *Prométhée* does justice (if only in a sketchy way) to Gide's demands on the novel as formulated in *Le Journal des Faux-Monnayeurs*: opinions exist only as functions of the character who expresses them (*J.d.F.-M.,* 13, 115); the "subject" is represented "objectivized" (to use Gide's own jargon [*ibid.,* 27]); the book gravitates around a number of centers (*ibid.,* 49); all "heroes" are orphans (by choice or circumstance) and bachelors (*ibid.,* 57); the narrative does not cling to "reality" (*ibid.,* 59f.), but exemplifies the *action gratuite et immotivée* (*ibid.,* 23), with a meaning in depth which hitherto has escaped the probing minds of the critics; it transposes the action onto a familiar, yet poeticized scene, slightly fantastic and supernatural, allowing certain *irréalités* to break into the narrative—a mythical scene, where the fable becomes timeless, attaining allegorical and symbolical dimensions (*ibid.,* 76). The deceptively simple style must appear to approach the most trivial forms of everyday language (*ibid.*, 80), so that by its very form alone the *Prométhée* illustrates William James's definition of all ideals on earth as always masked by the vulgarity of those circumstances which bring about their actualization—an aphorism greatly admired by Gide and entered in the *Journal des Faux-Monnayeurs* (43; July 22, 1921). The characters take their turn in the limelight, each one being briefly given a chance to express his own views (*ibid.*, 82). The novelist does not "direct the play," but listens as much as possible to his characters and watches them perform (*ibid.*, 84); rarely does he intervene and comment (*ibid.*, 80). Each character, in his own version, slightly deforms the events. The author's omniscience has given way to multilevel perspectivism (*ibid.*, 30f., 32). The characters' gestures spring from a confusing number of sources (*ibid.*, 46, 85).

The *Prométhée* even anticipates the moral lesson of *Les Faux-Monnayeurs*: from the "folly of the heroes" (*ibid.*, 81) which (*ridentem dicere verum*, "as truth laughingly told," Horace *Sat.* 1, 1, 24) conceals tragicomical problems, right down to the disquieting teachings of the novelist ("Inquiéter, tel est mon rôle," *J.d.F.-M.*, 95), whose questions calling in question everything, remain unanswerable, and whose literary *acte gratuit* sets into motion scandal (*skandalon*) the stumbling-block of a new morality outside the very confines of morality. Like all fictions of Gide, the *Prométhée* explores the unlimited possibilities of life, not the author's lived experience: it elevates the morality of a pseudomystical state of exalted expectation (*attente*)—in its way a religious, immoral, or creative pregnancy—above that of fulfillment (in life or literary creation), and places the value of striving above that of the goals which one may strive to attain (*ibid.*, 87). The *Prométhée*'s episodes and parables which ironically reflect each other (and upon each other) as well as its humorous puns, document the novelist's *disponibilité*, his openness, his availability for new literary experiments and adventures and for the scandalous ambiguities suggested by language itself. The gratuitous acts of language well up from the darkest regions of the subconscious, by the grace of associations and of a creative exhibitionism which tolerates no inhibitions. They are linguistic archetypes whose disquieting interplay permits the hermeneut to decipher the palimpsest below the surface of the scripture, the symbolic texture and structure which the text—*textus* and *textum*—text and fabric, simultaneously hides and reveals. The arbitrary gulf between content and form is bridged: they are born in language as if they were Siamese twins, inseparably linked together, and fed by the lifeblood of style. The word itself, creatively autonomous, mediates between ethos and aesthetics. Moral questions constitute topics, the mere "stuff" of books ("l'étoffe dont nos livres sont faits"); but morality being mere matter, it is subordinated to the creative principle of beauty. Ethos is reduced to "une dépendence de l'Esthétique" (*M.ch.*, 32), the latter with its capital *E* presenting the allegorical majesty of a pagan god on Olympus, towering high above the human frailties of Christian morals. Aesthetics, as it were, exacts remoteness—*le dépaysement*—distancing the actors from the audience, clearly delineating the boundary between nature and art; at the same time, alienation serves the surrealist transformation of reality to establish a mysterious bond which unites the personal neurosis of the spectator (or reader) with the psychotic world of the "hero," with his id, his ego, his libido, and a morality developed from Calvinist repressions. Gide's aesthetics rejects naturalistic imitations of an illusory "reality" which, even if it could succeed, "ne servirait qu'à faire, avec la réalité, pléonasme" (*ibid.*, 62f.). "Art is born of constraints, lives by combat, and dies through freedom" (*ibid.*, 64): Gide's artistic credo is that of a Nietzschean classicist. His art stands in inverse ratio to his morality, which thrives on absolute freedom and perishes under restraints. On one hand, the "immoralist's" striving for uncensored libertinage, for unlimited freedom of such mores as will guarantee the artist's and the individual's authenticity; on the other hand, the constraints without which art cannot exist: these are the polarities in tension which find expression in the paradoxes of Gide's œuvre. Aesthetically they aim at a sober banality, both in style and fable. Ethically they glorify the sovereign liberty of the individual, his right to shake off religious, social, and moral conventions, going so far as to exalt disinterested theft and murder as rigorous works of art (*Les Caves du Vatican*), and to defend the protagonist's corrupting complicity with the criminal (*L'Immoraliste*). Or else they may satirize unconscious hypocrisy, the religious rationalizations of libidinous drives (*La Symphonie pastorale*) or of sexual fears and insufficiencies (*La Porte étroite*), or the bondage of social and theological dogma (*Le Retour de l'enfant prodigue,* etc.).

Yet, despite his ostentatiously amoral attitudes, Gide, the man and the artist, remained a slave to the Puritanism of his earliest childhood. "[Je] compris," he wrote about 1896, "que la contrainte était chez moi plus naturelle que ne l'est chez d'autres l'abandon au plaisir" (*J.* 1, 105, *"Feuillets,"* 1896–). His entire œuvre bears witness to this ambivalence between a desire for absolute freedom in form and morals and discomfort in the face of this freedom—a discomfort deeply rooted in the Calvinist's irrepressible need for repressions, perhaps rationalized as the understanding that "de cette absence de liberté . . . venait la beauté de mes actes" (*ibid.*). The commandment of aesthetic hypocrisy, the constraint of the mask through which pierces symbolic truth, runs parallel to a desire for unrestrained expression of sacred and profane love, libidinous and emotional perversion. It also corresponds to an almost classicist need for constraints, for litotes, for acts and words whose meanings ambiguously reach far beyond their terseness and apparent triviality. These trends, far from slowly evolving, exist from the very beginning, together with all themes of Gide's fiction. The *Prométhée* testifies to the truth of Gide's remark to André Beaunier that the topics, the subject-matter of his major fiction, dated back to his very first days as a writer; the composition of the individual works—a mere problem of their sequence in time —often had to wait more than fifteen years. *Les Caves du Vatican*, for instance, was conceived while Gide was working on the *Prométhée*: "*Les Caves du Vatican* habitaient depuis plus de quinze ans dans ma tête, comme aussi j'y avais porté plus de quinze ans *la Porte étroite* et à peine un peu moins *L'Immoraliste*, premier sorti. Tous ces sujets se sont développés parallèlement, concurremment . . . Si j'avais pu, c'est *ensemble* que je les aurais écrits" (*J*. 1, 437; July 12, 1914).

3. The Sotie *as an Afterthought for a Farce on Divine Grace*

The *Prométhée* derives its aesthetic and moral unity from the nature of the *sotie*, Gide's lucky discovery long after the fact. The *Prométhée* became a *sotie* when Gide published (as a *sotie*) *Les Caves du Vatican* (1914). Into this period must have fallen his first encounter with sixteenth-century *soties*, to which Copeau may have introduced him. If lyricism penetrated the novel with Rousseau, epic poetry entered the lyric with Lamartine, Hugo, and Vigny. The mixture of the grotesque (even the absurd) and the tragicomic has permeated the French drama ever since Hugo; and while versification absorbs elements of prose, beginning with Baudelaire, the metaphysics of evil and the very problems of poetics are reflected in French poetry. Briefly, in the nineteenth century all clear lines of demarcation were broken down between the genres of French literature. Paradoxically, at the same rate at which the genres were mixed, attempts were made to preserve them in their "purity." Hence the reader must not be surprised by Gide's resolve to maintain the "purity" of the novel by transferring, fifteen years after the first edition, a work of narrative fiction, the *Prométhée*, to the realm of the *sotie*, which by definition belongs to the theatre. What was decisive here was not the genre in itself but rather a prevalent mood and tendency within a narrative which assumes the role of highly grotesque farce, an ironical mystery play that derides itself. The form rather than the genre was now determined by a dialectical topic of metaphysical proportions: the narrative dramatization of an apparently insoluble problem of theology. Narrative and dramatic dialogue, intermingled in the *Prométhée*, anticipate certain aspects of twentieth-century grotesque theatre (Beckett, Ionesco, Pinter, Albee, *et al.*).

Gide believed that every work of art evolves independently, according to an inherent aesthetic principle which the author may never fully comprehend or which may become intelligible to him decades after the act of creation. This belief explains Gide's belated realization that for two decades, up to 1914, the novelist had not yet produced a single true "novel"; what he now called *soties* and *récits* were purely ironical or didactic narratives: "Soties, récits, je n'ai jusqu'à présent écrit que des livres ironiques ou—critiques" (*J*. I, 437; July 12, 1914). Irony, criticism, didactic mystification, a Protestant delight in scandal, the wanton pranks of an *enfant terrible* in revolt against his Puritanism, a secretive sense of humor ("il lui faut [à l'artiste] une plaisanterie particulière; un drôle à lui" [*J*. I, 94, 1896]), mockery in the choice of his themes, seriousness in their artistic transformation and hidden ethos: these are the tendencies which in the *sotie* are concentrated to produce a literary paradox which corresponds to the puritanical and libidinous complexity, to the multivalent inversion (traceable right down to his syntax) of Gide the man and the artist: "Je ne suis qu'un petit garçon qui s'amuse—doublé d'un pasteur protestant qui l'ennuie" (*J.* I, 250; June 29, 1907).

What are *soties*? A synonym for *sottise, niaiserie, propos léger*, toward the end of the fifteenth century *sotie* (or *sottie*) lent its name to farces, where actors in fools' dress played allegorical roles with satirical significance. Related to the morality play, the *sotie* illustrated the Renaissance idea of the fool's freedom. Cryptically clad in the fool's motley, dangerous and unpleasant truths could be boldly expressed with impunity. I believe that the *sotie* is founded upon the Pauline concept of this world as the realm of foolishness (Rom. 1 : 22), where the faithful "are fools for Christ's sake" but "wise in Christ" (I Cor. 4 : 10): "If any man among you seemeth to be wise in the world, let him become a fool, that he may be wise" (I Cor. 3 : 18). Possibly an outgrowth of the ecclesiastic fool's revels (*festum stultorum, fatuorum*, or *follorum*), the *sotie* which flowered under Louis XII, satirized political, social, and religious situations—for example, the policies of Pope Julius II, which were inimical to the king of France (cf. Pierre Gringore, *Sottie contre le Pape Jules II*, where Gringore in the fool's dress of *la mère sotte* played in allegory the role of the Church). The anticlerical *Caves du Vatican* and the *sotie's* nature suggest that the buffooneries of the *Prométhée* were primarily meant to exemplify Gide's rupture with Calvinism, which at the turn of the century had become for him an aesthetic and moral necessity. On this emancipation, which determined not only the themes of his didactic art but also the free evolution of his homosexual trends, he declared in retrospect: "Et je ne sache pas qu'on puisse imaginer forme de pensée plus contraire à l'œuvre d'art (et à mon œuvre en particulier) et plus hostile même (le plus souvent sans le savoir) que le calvinisme. C'est là ce qui m'en a détaché dès le jour où j'ai pris la plume" (*J.* I, 298; April 24, 1910). The author of *Les Nourritures terrestres* (1897) found in the Scriptures the basis for his own hatred of the family as an institution ("Familles, je vous hais!") as well as for the hostility that Ménalque (the redeeming tempter-figure of the *Nourritures*) feels toward tradition, inheritance, disciples, and epigones ("Nathanaël, jette ce livre!"). To Gide's mind, Christ's contempt for all family and social ties was disregarded by the Apostles in their dogmatic teachings (cf. *J.* I, 96, "Morale chrétienne," 1896–). Gide's harsh criticism is directed against the petrification of Christ's living ideas in Christian doctrine. Quoting Schiller's *Braut von Messina* (III, 5): "Und alles ist Frucht, und alles ist Samen" ("and all is fruit, and all is seed"), he comments: "Mais catholicisme d'abord, protestantisme ensuite, après avoir été formules expansives, sont formules restrictives depuis longtemps . . . n'importe quelle formule de n'importe quelle religion ne peut être considérée que comme appelée à disparaître. Nul plus que le Christ n'a ruiné de ces formules usées" (*J.* I, 95). These ideas are transposed into a grotesque allegory in *Histoire de Tityre*, a parable told by Prometheus within the framework of Gide's *Prométhée*. The work of art is the exaggeration of an idea, the symbol is at the root of the book, the book is not mere literature (i.e., dead letter) but *un sac de graines* (*J.* I, 93f.): man's task consists in the stage-management of ideas on earth ("la mise en scène des idées sur la terre"), for "nous n'avons de valeur que *représentative*" (*ibid.,* 92; cf. *Paludes*, 126). These entries in Gide's diaries, entitled *Littérature et morale*, again demonstrate the close links which existed between his aesthetic, religious, and moral preoccupations: his literary conscience, his puritanical strife for stylistic and structural perfection, seem almost unthinkable without his religious scruples and mystifications. What he sees as the theatrical mission of mankind on earth is the enactment of an *illusion*: man must "appear" in order to "be" (*paraître pour être*), he must act not by way of mimesis, not directing or performing an imitation of "reality," but by incarnating an idea, a symbol, an allegory. He must exaggerate the *sotie*, the fool's play and farce of moral concepts, translating them into the trivialities of everyday language and happenings, so that they strike the imagination with the full impact of their scandalous absurdity. Gide's *sotie* uses myth to stimulate thought, for he conceives of myth as "addressing itself primarily and solely to reason. The Greek fable is essentially sensible [*raisonnable*]," he taught in the fragment of the *Dioscures* (*Inc.*, 126, first published incomplete in the September 1919 issue of the *Nouvelle Revue française*). For Gide, it is easier to believe in the rational truth of Greek myth, or rather in his own rationalizations of it, than in the doctrine of St. Paul: "dont le propre est précisément de soumettre, supplanter, 'abêtir' et assermenter la raison" (*ibid.*). Gide is amazed by the inconsistencies of Protestantism: "Je m'étonne que le protestantisme, en repoussant les hiérarchies de l'Eglise, n'ait pas repoussé du même coup les oppressantes institutions de saint Paul, le dogmatisme de ses épîtres" (*J.* 1, 96, 1896–). Paul, Luther, and Calvin conceal God's truth and, exalting the divine superego, fail to see Christ's emancipation of the id, his word which liberates man from fear and guilt. "Entre lui [le Christ] et moi, je tiens Calvin ou saint Paul pour deux écrans également néfastes," Gide wrote in the draft for a preface to *La Symphonie pastorale* (*J.* 1, 300, 1910), and monotonously he repeated in his diaries (1911): "Qu'il ait nom saint Paul, Luther, Calvin, je sens à travers lui toute la vérité de Dieu se ternir" (*J.* 1, 342). Gide's unorthodox Protestantism, *protesting* against clerical institutions, dogma, and "authorities"—and above all against Paul, Luther, and Calvin—culminates in the poetic creation of a private hermeneutics; it allows the author to play his own, very personal, problems through the masks of his characters and to preach seriously through the rational *plaisanteries particulières* of his grotesque myths his gospel of hatred against family ties and all traditional doctrines of Christian theology.

The moral problem so derisively treated in the *Prométhée* appeared first in Gide's diary in the form of a quotation from Bossuet's *Panégyrique de Sainte Thérèse*: " '. . . Ou souffrir, ou mourir—*Aut pati, aut mori*. Il est digne de votre audience de comprendre solidement toute la force de cette parole; . . . vous confesserez avec moi qu'elle renferme comme en a-brégé toute la doctrine du Fils de Dieu, et tout l'esprit du christianisme.' Et plus loin: 'il n'est rien de plus opposé que de vivre selon la nature et de vivre selon la grâce.' " Gide's commentary was brief and damning: "Tant pis!" (*J.* I, 90f., 1896). There is a relationship working both ways between Gide's laconic commentary and the grotesque didacticism of the *Prométhée*; the *sotie* was conceived about that time. According to its author, it had cleared the way for the composition of *Le Roi Candaule* (1899-1901), producing a catharsis similar to the one effected a few years later by *L'Immoraliste* and saving the sanity of Gide the man: "Sans mon *Prométhée*, mon *Candaule* en fût resté tout encombré et sans mon *Immoraliste*, je risquais de le devenir," Gide wrote to Francis Jammes on February 6, 1902, adding, "Je me purge" (*Corr. F.J.-A.G.*). With the aid of the *Prométhée*, Gide temporarily succeeded in purging himself from his Calvinist nightmare by banning it into the frivolous pages of his *sotie*, which contains the hidden message of this-worldly Christianity. The latter proved durable beyond all expectations, largely no doubt because of its theatrical potential on which he could draw for striking impressive poses. In this respect, the final paragraph of *Numquid et tu* . . . ? (*J.* 1, 605, 1914-1919) is revealing, summing up once more the *Prométhée*'s moral lessons.[7] To this scriptural theme Gide still harked back in 1935, at the height of his rather ambiguous Communist commitment: "J'ai été frappé, dans la lecture de l'Evangile, par ces mots 'et nunc' qui s'y répètent constamment" (*Litt. eng.*, 69).

The passage from Bossuet and Gide's commentary are indeed useful for an interpretation of the *Prométhée*: the sufferings of the self-satisfied Coclès, who believes in his natural bounty, finding himself *trop naturellement bon* (310), call for a Pauline rebuke: "But the natural man receiveth not the things of the Spirit of God" (1 Cor. 2 : 14). The eagle, Prometheus's conscience which feeds on his vitality, and Damoclès's sickness unto death, caused by a playful *acte gratuit* with which Zeus, the banker, bestows upon him a grace that he cannot accept—*gratia irresistibilis* ("irresistible grace") without which *donum perseverantiae* ("the gift of perseverance") proves inefficient: Damoclès is "called" but not "chosen" ("for many be called, but few chosen," Matt. 20 : 16). In the fragment on the Dioscures, Gide explains that the heroes of Greek antiquity are destroyed not by an external fate, but by an inner, psychological, fatality (*Inc.*, 127). The foolish antiheroes of the *Prométhée* owe their absurdity and alienation to a fate that pursues them from without as Zeus's *actes gratuits* which correspond to no inner necessity. It seems to destroy Damoclès—but perhaps it mysteriously redeems

---

[7] "*Il vient une heure*, ET ELLE EST DÉJÀ VENUE, dit le Christ. . . . *Venit hora*, ET NUNC EST. Celui qui attend cette heure par delà de la mort l'attend en vain. Dès l'heure où tu nais de nouveau, dès l'instant où tu bois de cette eau, tu entres dans le Royaume de Dieu, tu prends part à la vie éternelle. *En vérité, en vérité, je vous le dis*, répète partout le Christ, *celui qui écoute ma parole* A (non pas: aura mais *a déjà*) LA VIE ÉTERNELLE. . . *Il passe de la mort à la vie. Transiit a morte in vitam* (John 5 : 24).

him—while Coclès appears to escape its fatal effects, thanks to Prometheus's liberating act of salvation. But nothing can be said with certainty about the nature of these "last things"; in the eschatological *sotie*, Calvinist "predestination" (and the multiple perspective of Gide's narrative art) may keep their dark arcana, their inviolable secrets. "J'aime . . . que chaque livre porte en lui, mais cachée, sa propre réfutation et ne s'assoie pas sur l'idée, de peur qu'on n'en voie l'autre face," declares Gide in the postlude to the second edition of *Paludes* (1479).

4. A Note on the Prometheus Topos

It would go beyond the scope of this study if I attempted to summarize the extensive research that has been devoted to the Prometheus myth in its manifold modern interpretations. For a detailed account of the metamorphoses of Prometheus in European sacred and profane literature, the reader may repair to Raymond Trousson's *Le Thème de Prométhée dans la littérature européenne*.[8] Treating all modern aspects of the Prometheus myth, this monumental work provides keen insights into the identification of the Titan with Christ, which occurs most vividly in Edgar Quinet's *Prométhée* (1838) (cf. Trousson, 74ff.). Trousson is somewhat disappointing in the interpretation of Gide's *Prométhée* (Trousson, 435-438), basing himself largely on secondary sources. Of particular interest for my exegesis is Trousson's chapter 2, "Prometheus-Christus?" which traces Romantic and post-Romantic fusions of Prometheus with Christ to a badly misunderstood (and in this misunderstanding literarily fertile) passage in Tertullian (*Adversus Marcionem* 1.1.247; cf. Trousson, 73ff.).

[8] 2 vols., Geneva, 1964.

In addition to Trousson, a selective bibliography may suffice to dispel some of the doubts which the reader may bring
to my exegesis of Gide's *Prométhée*.[9] It would, of course, be

[9] For the tradition which underlies eighteenth- and nineteenth-century interpretations of the Promethean myth see the following works.
On Prometheus-Logos as an allegory for life-giving thought and its
creative utterance—the conjunction of *sapientia* and *eloquentia*—and
on the abstract modifications of this metaphor by Protagoras, Isocrates,
and Cicero, as well as on its survival through Alcuin and John of
Salisbury to Juan Luis Vives, see R. Johnson, "The Promethean Com-
monplace," *Journal of the Warburg and Courtauld Institutes*, xxv
(1962), 9-17 (hereafter referred to as *JWCI*). On the transferal of a
Trinitarian series of creation myths (Prometheus, Mercury, Minerva,
respectively Prometheus, Mercury, the Parcae) from pagan sarcophagi
to early Christian ones, with reference to Augustine, see J. P. Migne,
Patrologia Latina, xxxiv, col. 291, 128; xxxii, col. 817; xxxviii, col.
703; xl, col. 167; cf. Adelheid Heimann, "Trinitas Creator Mundi,"
JWCI, ii (1938-1939), 43ff. On Prometheus as a prefiguration of God
and Christ, and on other metamorphoses of the Promethean myth up
to the eighteenth century, see Olga Raggio, "The Myth of Prometheus,"
JWCI, xxi (1958), 44-62. On Prometheus as a Christ figure in the
work of Piero di Cosimo, see Erwin Panofsky, *Studies in Iconology*
(New York, 1939), pp. 55-56, where a parallel is drawn between the
theological division of human history into the eras *ante legem*, *sub
lege*, and *sub gratia*, and into the eras *ante Vulcanum*, *sub Vulcano*,
and *sub Prometheo*: "the analogy of ideas holds good to the extent that
in both cases the inaugurator of the third phase is crucified for those
whom he was destined to save."
    For the tradition of the eagle or vulture of Prometheus, see Servius
on *Caucaseasque refert volucres furtumque Promethei* (*Eclogue* 6. 42)
in *P. Vergilii Maronis Opera cum Commentariis* (Venice, 1538):
Servius sees in the eagle (or vulture) a symbol of the worries besetting
Prometheus's heart. Claude Mignault, in his commentary on Emblem
CII in Alciati, *Emblemata* (Paris, 1618), p. 465, confuses Prometheus
with Tityus when he refers to Macrobius, *Commentarii in Somnium
Scipionis* (1. 10, 12), where the bird of prey tormenting Tityus represents, like the one in Gide's *Prométhée*, "tormenta malae conscien-
tiae."
    For an understanding of the Prometheus figure in English Romanti-
cism, see Christian Kreutz, *Das Prometheussymbol in der Dichtung der
englischen Romantik* (Göttingen, 1963)—more valuable for its bibliography than for its rather pedestrian interpretation—and Oskar Wal-

absurd to assume that Gide knew any of these specialized studies, some of which were published after his death, all of them after the *Prométhée*. Like most scholarly endeavors, they serve as posthumous documentation for a tradition of which artists, poets, and writers are aware throughout the ages, without knowing its precise details.

Keeping in mind this distinction, I add that the Gide of the 1890s—an avid reader of Goethe and the English Romantics—was familiar with Goethe's *Prometheus* fragment (1770s) and with its interpretation in *Dichtung und Wahrheit* (III, 15). The cursory appearance of Prometheus's mistress, Asie, testifies to Gide's knowledge of Shelley's *Prometheus Unbound*. Prometheus, the gods' equal, the mediator, the Logos, the creator of man, not a subaltern figure like Milton's Satan, yet a rebel and savior in revolt against Jupiter's law: this seems to be Goethe's contribution to Gide's protagonist. It is enhanced by the rebellious Christ typos that, for example, F. A. Lea believed he had found in Shelley's Prometheus: "Prometheus is intended to be a second Christ."[10]

In his creative use of the Prometheus typos, Gide combines elements of the early Christian, Renaissance, pre-Romantic, and Romantic commonplaces—traditional aspects of the Titan as they survive in the eighteenth and nineteenth centuries, requiring on the part of the author a certain amount of literacy but no specific erudition—with very private associations derived from his puritanical upbringing, against which he revolts while paradoxically holding on to

---

zel, *Das Prometheussymbol von Shaftesbury bis Goethe*, 3rd ed. (Munich, 1932), a short study which provides keen insights into the transformation of Shaftesbury's Prometheus image by the German enlightenment, the *Storm and Stress*, and the German Romantics.

[10] F. A. Lea, *Shelley and the Romantic Revolution* (London, 1945), p. 194.

them as a nigh inexhaustible reservoir of themes for the novelist.

5. Symbol and Allegory

Gide's *Prométhée* is neither a modernized version nor a parody of the myth of Prometheus. It is a modern allegory in which the repetitive pattern of allusions, images, and figurative sequences constitutes a qualitative progression, replacing the traditional system of narrative progression.

Gide's Titan comes to life in an equally symbolic and allegorical struggle with his eagle (or vulture): a conflict which after long suffering terminates in the joyous consumption of the divine bird of prey. As a symbol—pointing beyond Prometheus, the maker of Man and the fire-thief, to a multivalence of significations, all simultaneous with and transcending the Prometheus myth—Gide's protagonist embodies those attributes which turn him into an allegory, in both meanings of the word: the personification of an abstract idea, and the central character of a mystery play about the elusive sense of this incarnate abstraction. Prometheus, the allegory of the savior of mankind, the supernatural thief and donor of the divine fire (which gives life to humankind) is an analogy of Christ and a moral parable on the elusiveness of Christ's teaching.

One example may suffice, at this point, to illustrate Gide's allegorizing procedure. It consists in the use of banal everyday phrases which conceal an unsuspected anagogical analogy, the trivial metaphor pointing ironically towards a metaphysical or theological truth which goes far beyond its surface meaning. Prometheus mysteriously answers the aggressive *garçon*, who insists on learning what he does (or did in the past), that he used to make matches (*des allumettes*, 307), a dark allusion not only to the theft of fire ("I have come to send fire on the earth," Luke 12 : 49), but also to the teasing effect (*allumer*) of the somewhat ambivalent meaning of the Incarnate Word. Concluding that his guest no longer does anything, the ministering *garçon* says, "Alors mettons: homme de lettres" (307), a dual pun which hides and reveals that for him Prometheus is the Incarnate Word (the "man made of letters," "incarnate word") which the *garçon* will pronounce (*alors mettons*, "let us say")—but as the scriptural letter, not its spirit. Etymologically, Prometheus is prescience. The skeptical crowd sees in his eagle at best a "conscience" ("tout au plus une conscience," 314), συνείδησις ("conscience"), the judge who knows good and evil, "God's interpreter" (according to Philo Judaeus) and, if one believes Luther, the wild beast which rouses man against himself. According to Kant (after Philo Judaeus), the eagle is "the consciousness of an inner court of justice." In short, he is both conscience and consciousness. For Gide (who discovered Nietzsche about this time), these were the antivital powers par excellence, inimical to all sound instincts. Prometheus's eagle is as undesirable a gift from an obsessive superego as are the five hundred francs which the same banker Zeus, by a whimsical "act of grace," has destined for Damoclès, and which will prove fatal. Damoclès tries in vain to get rid of a treasure which oppresses and finally crushes him because he knows that he has not earned it. Prometheus and his eagle represent the enigmatical intertwinings of *praescientia* ("foreknowledge") and *conscientia* ("conscience and consciousness"), of an external fate and the inner fatality of a guilt complex that undermines life, of absurdly disproportionate guilt feelings and a grace so mysterious and arbitrary that it can easily be mistaken for a punishment (cf. Gide on Oedipus and Prometheus, *J*. 1, 342, "Feuillets," 1911–).

In similar fashion all characters of the *Prométhée* are enacting a satirical allegory of Calvinist concepts of anguish, guilt, punishment, predestination, undeserved grace (or lack of grace), freedom, and self-imposed *contraintes*. I maintain that Gide's moral and aesthetic problems in the 1890s are translated into the dramatic farce of the *Prométhée*. The *sotie* paradoxically presents his anti-Pauline Protestantism in Pauline gestures of self-dramatization, the tensions of Gide the libertine at odds with Gide the Puritan whose anticlerical and this-worldly "Christianity" is reconciled with a taste for pederasty and for the Arcadia of Virgil's *Bucolics*. Aesthetically it expresses his artistic asceticism, the classicist rigor of stylistic understatement, purism, the cult of *le mot juste mais vague*, counterbalanced by the narcissism of Gide the descendant of Romanticism, and the private associations of Gide the disciple of Mallarmé in revolt against his master's voice.

Gide's incessant preoccupation with the purity of the genre "novel" is reflected in his wavering attitude toward the designation that might be given the *Prométhée*: he first announces it as a novel (*roman*) in *L'Ermitage* (1899) but publishes it in book form with the Mercure de France without any indication of genre (1899). In *Saül* (1903) it is again advertised as *roman*. The discovery of the *sotie*—a term first applied to *Les Caves du Vatican* (1914)—solves the problem of the *Prométhée*'s genre once and for all. As *sotie*, the *Prométhée* is even brought to the stage by Renée and Arnold Naville (1928).

The cryptic term *sotie*, so unusual in a modern context, in the end was found ideal, since it could embrace a contemporary mystery play and mystification, symbolic but subtly ironizing Symbolism itself, and satire of a Protestant ethos which—within the confines of the *Prométhée*—is at once exorcized and celebrated in repetitive patterns of episodes whose widening (or narrowing) cycles represent the tempo of its progression.

One. A DIVINE GRATUITY, OR THE MISFORTUNES OF THE ELECT

1. Exposition, Characters, and Literary Climate of the Prométhée

THE MEANING of the *Prométhée* logically derives from an exposition which precedes it in the form of a prologue. A sort of slapstick prelude, it is narrated dispassionately, dryly reported without commentary like a *fait divers*: "On the boulevard which leads from the Madeleine to the Opéra," a fat gentleman drops his handkerchief. A lean man picks it up, runs after the fat one and returns it to him. The fat gentleman gives the lean one a flask with "portable ink," a pen, and an envelope, inviting him to address it to a "name" he knows. After having put a five hundred franc note into the envelope, the fat gentleman slaps the lean one so powerfully that he falls down. The fat gentleman leaves the scene in a cab. Bleeding heavily, the lean man rises again and testily tells the worried audience that he barely felt anything, and asks them if they will please leave him alone. Now the author intervenes with the casual remark that he subsequently learned the fat gentleman was Zeus, the banker. The identity of the ill-treated lean man and that of the "elect" so whimsically chosen is slowly revealed in the *sotie*'s first part ("La moralité privée"); the former is Coclès, the latter Damoclès.

The complex structure of part I, "Chronique de la moralité privée," introduces, one by one, the characters of the *sotie*. The scene is a Parisian café on the *grands boulevards*. Chance and necessity are intertwined in the meeting of the *garçon*, Prometheus, Damoclès, and Coclès. Each character, with

35

the exception of the transcendent "Miglionnaire" Zeus, is given his turn in the limelight: "Histoire du garçon et du Miglionnaire" (304), told by the *garçon*; "Histoire de Damoclès" (308); "Histoire de Coclès" (310); "Prométhée parle" (313); "Histoire de l'aigle" (314). To this perspectivism corresponds the precipitous action of a farce of errors, interspersed with the protagonists' "stories" or speeches, within the framework of the sections numbered one to four: a dual web of structures illustrating by their very nature the incommunicability of a nigh Kafkaesque morality authored by the "Miglionnaire" Zeus. Part I ends in the midst of confusion and misunderstandings with apocalyptic overtones which will be analyzed in the course of this exegesis.

The intricacies of the *Prométhée*'s dual structure, studied in detail by W. W. Holdheim,[1] are carried over into parts II, III and IV. Part II, "La Détention de Prométhée," Prometheus, denounced by the *garçon* and imprisoned, receives the *garçon*, who informs him about the changing fortunes of Damoclès and Coclès. Prometheus feeds his eagle, demonstrating its "morality," in the chapter headed "Il faut qu'il croisse et que je diminue." Prometheus escapes by means of his eagle. He then gives his lecture on everyone's eagle, ultimately begging the question in the chapter entitled "La Pétition de principes." Damoclès catches a cold when leaving the lecture hall.

Part III, "La Maladie de Damoclès," shows the rise of Coclès (who had lost one eye to the eagle at the end of Part I) and the decline of Damoclès (who on that same memorable occasion had thought that he had paid for all and everything). Damoclès dies and is buried. The whole sequence of events is enigmatically punctuated by an "Interview du Miglionnaire," given to Prometheus and the *garçon* (328ff.).

Part IV, "Histoire de Tityre," is a parable told by Prome-

[1] *Theory and Practice of the Novel* (Geneva, 1968), pp. 190ff.

theus in lieu of a funeral oration for Damoclès. The story of
Tityre's fixed idea, implanted by Ménalque, which grows together with a tree planted by Ménalque in Tityre's swamp so
that both become an overpowering obsession, illustrates the
futility of human efforts to decipher transcendent messages.
The parabolic truth of "Histoire de Tityre" (and of the *Prométhée* as a whole) is confirmed by the joyful consumption of
the eagle (by Prometheus, Coclès, and the *garçon*), and by
the author's cryptic postscript, in the form of an epilogue,
on the inscrutability of acts and creations which go beyond
human intentions.

The four parts of the *Prométhée* demonstrate the disquieting consequences of the dramatic prelude in numerous
episodes in which Prometheus and the *garçon* act as inter-
cessors. By telling his eagle's story (and history) and the
parable of Tityre's tree, Prometheus shows in a glass darkly
the *moralité privée* of the central fable. The sober objectivity
of the prelude, the "realist" narratives of absurd and grotesque circumstances, and the naturalism and gothic humor
of the strange happenings burlesque themselves, testifying to
loss of innocence in novelistic narcissism by way of the irony
which now permeates the novel's aesthetics and structure.
Three features of the *Prométhée* are in flagrant contradiction
with objectivity, the mimetic "realism," and the "naturalistic"
sobriety of its style. First, there are the alienated characters,
a strangely eclectic group assembled from Sicilian and Roman legendary history (Damoclès and Coclès), Greek mythology (Zeus, Prometheus, the eagle), modern finance and
even restaurants (Zeus, the banker and "Miglionnaire," and
the *garçon* who ministers to the culinary needs of his guests).
Protagonists emerging at the same time from Gide's previous
works (*Paludes*, *Les Nourritures terrestres*) and Virgil's
Eclogues (Tityre, Moelibée, Ménalque), these characters allude to the economic, medical, and alimentary vocabulary

of the Christian doctrines of salvation. Secondly, there is
the hidden supernaturalism of the "happenings," which are
narrated in "naturalistic" terms or occur as dialogues in trivial
everyday language. And thirdly, time and place (May 189–,
the Parisian *grands boulevards*, the *salle des nouvelles lunes*)
incorporate *hic et nunc*, here and now, the grotesque episodes
of the *sotie*, and yet convey the timelessness of myth as well
as the real scene, which is transformed by it.

2. The Ambiguities of "mal enchaîné" and "la moralité privée"

In the themes of the *Prométhée* Gide stages mystery, sacrament, self-denial, martyrdom, and the secret of sacrifice in
the form of a farcical mystification of matters of faith, grace,
predestination, and Eucharist. Originally mystification represented the typological correlation between sensuous symbol
and the object it symbolized. Mystery equals sacrament ("sacramentum vel mysterium");[2] a sacred act is almost the equivalent of sacrifice in Augustine's definition ("quasi sacrum
facere"); and, according to Isidore of Seville, it corresponds
to "secret" ("sacrum = secretum").[3]

Mystery and mystification begin with the very title of the
Prométhée, with the ambiguities hidden in the words *mal
enchaîné*. First, they suggest that the *Prométhée* is logically
poor (*mal enchaîné*) in its formal structure, as at first glance
it may appear with its confusing *tiroirs*, its anecdotes within
episodes and narratives, its dual structure of chapters over-
flowing from one numbered section into the next one. Secondly, logically poor (*mal enchaîné*) too is Prometheus's prescience regarding the unpredictable reactions which the
"banker's" playful *acte gratuit* produces in the meditative

[2] Lubac, *Corpus mysticum*, 2nd ed. (Paris, 1949), p. 56.
[3] *Ibid.*, p. 55.

Damoclès and Coclès, the man of works, owing to their
(rather limited) free will. Finally, *mal enchaîné*, "poorly
bound," Prometheus descends from the Caucasus, proving
his ubiquity by appearing incognito in a Parisian café. Although he can free himself of Zeus's gift, for a long time he
prefers to his freedom the eagle that feeds on his vital substance, the devouring beast that is his cross, his suffering,
his love—his passion. Ambiguously the eagle is at the same
time the divine side that consumes his humanity and the human congregation gnawing at his divine substance. "Il faut
qu'il croisse et que je diminue," Prometheus reflects on his
bird of prey (317), using (like Tityre, the author-hero of
Paludes [126]) the words of John the Baptist at the baptism
of Christ, "He must increase, and I must decrease" (John
3 : 30). As long as the eagle remains external, Prometheus's
divinity is unfulfilled; it is actualized in the Eucharist, the
banquet of life in the company of Coclès and the *garçon*
where the eagle is eaten in Holy Communion, *et nunc*, bringing eternal life to the body of the community. As so often in
nineteenth-century literature (and already in Goethe's *Prometheus* fragment of 1774), the redeemer of mankind appears as a synthesis of Lucifer and Messiah, impotent in his
intercession with a jealous God who scorns, persecutes, and
punishes him with the vindictiveness of a suspicious superego. Prometheus, the redeemer-tempter, prefers to man that
which devours man: "Je n'aime pas les hommes; j'aime ce
qui les dévore" (322). In this he resembles Zeus, who shows
a sardonically clinical interest not in Damoclès the man but
in his fatal disease (328). By what is man devoured? By his
quest for self-fulfillment and identity, not by his pursuit of
happiness. As the *garçon* explains to Prometheus, the crowd
is searching for its personality on the "boulevard qui mène de
la Madeleine à l'Opéra"—the broad road of sin which from
the church of the forgiven sinner (Madeleine symbolizing

Mary Magdalene) leads to operative grace, and where in
the prelude Coclès, too, had tried to find happiness—"Ce
qu'ils cherchent, c'est leur personnalité . . . ce que nous appelons ici, idiosyncrasie" (304). They have "no continuing
city" here "but . . . seek one to come" (Heb. 13 : 14). What
the crowd seeks cannot be obtained by external means of
grace: it is that *gratia operans* ("operative grace") which in
mysterious ways effects a person's innermost self, working
through his idiosyncrasies which he may never fully discover.
The descent of the (lifted up) Prometheus ("The Son of
Man must be lifted up," John 3 : 14) takes place outside
time, or rather in pagan cyclic time, seasonally: "entre quatre
et cinq heures d'automne" (304). Coclès and Damoclès, however, are situated in time, in history: Coclès, *natural* man,
good *before* the fall, enters historical time after the fall when
he reflects for the first time on good and evil: "Et si ce n'est
pas par erreur—pensai-je, car pour la première fois je pensais; si
ce soufflet m'était bien destiné!" (311) Coclès with his temporal, linear existence can ask himself whether he owes his
fall to *predestination* or rather to a *mistake* (a sin), just as
Damoclès during the remainder of his earthly life can doubt
his "call" since it merely came to him as a matter of chance
(*fortuitement*, 310, 311). Prometheus alone can proclaim his
extemporality, his existence outside history: "Vous avez
chacun votre histoire; je n'en ai pas" (313). Only when the
time is ripe and harvest at hand does he appear symbolically,
at the hour of the last supper whose reenactment connects
the old Adam with the new man. In his sacramental con-
cealment Prometheus remains incognito, unrecognizable.

"Chronique de la moralité privée," the subheading of the
Prométhée's first part, ambiguously hints at the sacral farce
of the arcana of predestination and free will: the "private
morality" of the *acte gratuit* as the Augustinian *gratia gratis
data*, a free act of divine grace which—undeserved and whim-

sical—goes counter to the expectations of public morality. Canceling out the concept of grace as the effect of good works, it deprives morality of its rewards, of its meaning. Hence, *la moralité privée* reveals a second hidden sense: it is "bereft of morality," or "morality abolished." Where an arbitrary act of grace predetermines before birth who will be among the elect, there too begins a mysterious and mystifying (*privée*) morality which is no longer justifiable by reason. It is the Pauline "il faut s'abêtir" of Pascal, stagnation in a pool of bad conscience, feelings of guilt and unfulfilled duties; it is self-hatred counteracting that continuous renewal of the self which for Gide is the true meaning of the Christian doctrine of redemption *et nunc* (John 6, *passim*) and which he still understands a quarter of a century later as the promise of a state of paradisiacal joy, here and now: "L'état de joie dont nous parle le Christ est un état, non point futur mais immédiat" (Dostoïevsky, 207).

3. The Vexations of Divine Grace and of Man's Gratuitous Actions

Mystery and mystification: To Prometheus (whom he does not recognize) the *garçon* explains the mystery of the *acte gratuit*, Coclès's rather unpleasant encounter with Zeus: a sort of pentecostal happening (it takes place in May) on the broad road between sin and operating grace; a descent of the Holy Spirit which at first seems to work against natural man (Coclès) in favor of the apparently "chosen" (but only "called") Damoclès, but which subsequently seems to reverse its action; a mystery which the *garçon* fails to comprehend although he attempts to explain what little he understands of it. In the *garçon's* description this *acte gratuit* only admits a fideist interpretation. It must be accepted as a matter of faith and escapes rational cognition. In the *garçon's* own terms, it occurred "without a motive," "irrationally" (*sans motif, sans raison,* 305), "born of itself" (*né de soi,* 305), a truly "disinterested act" (*l'acte désintéressé,* 305), "without finality" (*l'acte aussi sans but,* 305) and hence without a master (*donc sans maître,* 305). Spontaneously generated, the *acte gratuit* is "free" (*l'acte libre,* 305), an unrequested gift (*l'Acte autochthone,* 305). Autochthonous in its allegorical divinity (implied by its capitalization), it potentially has the power of an entelechy which may or may not actualize potential grace in some one "called" but not necessarily "chosen." "J'étais quelconque, je suis quelqu'un," and "cette aventure me détermine," declares Damoclès (310) most unhappy about the course of events which determines his unbidden "idiosyncrasy" as well as his fate. He misunderstands the possible salvation which his new state of unfreedom might bring him; likewise he fails to comprehend the decisive role of his will to resist, his *posse resistere,* his willful ingratitude (born of ignorance and annihilating grace), which too was a free gift of operative grace[4] bestowed upon him by a divine irony cruel in its mystifying mysteries. One begins to see why Zeus is a banker: his gifts are illusory, they are merely *loans*—"Mon jeu c'est de prêter aux hommes . . . je prête, mais c'est avec l'air de donner" (329). The owner of a banking establishment to which all mankind consciously or unknowingly is indebted, Zeus is also the banker at the cosmic gambling-table of grace where he keeps a bank that no one can break.

---

[4] *Gratis,* "free," a contraction of *gratiis,* "by grace." My interpretation of the Gidean *acte gratuit* seems to be borne out by the example of Lafcadio's reasoning about his *crime immotivé* (829), the murder of Anthime Fleurissoire: an act perpetrated, in a Nietzschean sense, "beyond good and evil" (822), in a Pascalian vein, a *pari* (*pour la grâce,* 831), and on a broader, cosmological level, a Mallarméan *coup de dés* [*qui*] *jamais n'abolira le hasard,* executed by a sort of *demi-dieu* in a limbo outside Christianity and steeped in an ambiguous atmosphere between myth and reality, not unlike *Zeus-le-Banquier-Miglionnaire.* (Cf. *Les Caves du Vatican,* 821ff.)

Zeus's omnipotence, the sadistic cat-and-mouse game of his
impenetrable acts of grace which destroy the skeptic Damoclès (who has no reason to believe himself "chosen" or even
"called"), Zeus's cynical gambler's nature, capable only of
winning, seem like a parody of the almost monotheistic Zeus
of Aeschylus. Simultaneously his agnomen "le Miglionnaire"
with its pseudo-Italian beginning ("Miglion-") points to
ultramontane (Roman) origins, while its ending ("-naire")
hints on one hand at the vernacular French, the language of
the Reformed cult, and on the other hand at the four Gallican articles drawn up by Bossuet in 1682, the third of which
insisted that the ancient privileges of the Gallican Church
were inviolable: dark allusions which bring to mind the Bossuet quotation in Gide's diary (*J.* I, 90f., 1896)—so close to
Calvinism—which we have cited as a text correlated with the
morality of the *Prométhée.* The word (or nonword) "Miglionnaire," derived from "million," an augmentative form
of "mille," also puns upon "millénaire," the "millennium,"
while Zeus's uncommon corporeal substance (*sa peu commune corpulance,* 303) and his indefinite age (*entre deux
âges,* 303) metaphorically indicate this god's role between
two aeons. "Je suis riche, bien plus que l'on ne peut l'imaginer. Tu es à moi," he prides himself, speaking to Prometheus,
and pointing to the *garçon:* "Il est à moi; tout est à moi"
(328). His infinite riches and health, his dubious monetary
gift which like a sword hangs over Damoclès's head tormenting him unto sickness and death, the correlations between
duties, debts (*dettes, devoirs*) and failing health correspond
to the medical and economic vocabulary of Christian salvation.[5]

---

[5] "οἰκονομία, *oeconomia*": in Ambrose, Jerome, Origen, Cassian, and
other Church fathers, "plan of salvation," "incarnation (of the divine
Word)"; *salus,* "health" and "wealth," "eternal life"; *redemptio,*
"repurchase," "redemption" (in a commercial and then in a spiritual

Mystery and mystification: the *garçon* understands as little about the nature of Zeus and the supernatural problems of grace and predestination as Coclès and Damoclès, who are made to suffer through them; yet he humbly admires and accepts them as inscrutable matters of faith. Throughout the *Prométhée* the *garçon* plays the role of a mediator between the natural and the supernatural. In fact he holds the office of a minister. As such he remains anonymous. It is not his name, but his office alone that is important: *garçon* "waiter," in Latin, *minister*[6]—a priest of the Reformed cult. He administers the three Calvinist sacraments: the Last Supper (307), baptism (312) and absolution (to the dying Damoclès) (333). *Minister verbi Dei*, as minister of God's word he propagates the good word, talks to Zeus and intercedes with him, vaguely divines the nature of this *Deus ignotus*, the unknown God who does not reveal himself to reason and whose medical and financial services save only the believer, bringing damnation to the infidel. Although during Damoclès's fatal illness Zeus daily asks the *garçon* for news about the patient's health, he does not answer this minister's fervent prayers to make himself known to the anguished sufferer. "Damoclès guérirait pourtant s'il connaissait son bienfaiteur," the worried *garçon* confides in Prometheus. "Je le lui dis [à Zeus], mais il persiste, veut garder son incognito" (328). "Zeus incognito, Deus ignotus": like Calvin's God, Zeus is interested in evil, in Damoclès's sin, not in the

---

sense), "ransom"; *perditio*, "bankruptcy," and, metaphorically, "damnation," "eternal death"; *salvatio*, originally "healing," "cure," and, according to Ficino, "wealth," "financial security"—significant because of Damoclès's strange destiny; *damnum* in its primitive meaning of "loss," an antonym for *lucrum, incrementum*, and of some interest in view of Coclès's loss of an eye and its replacement by a glass eye.

[6] In the Pauline sense of the word, "ut sim minister Christi" (Rom. 15 : 16), "minister fidelis" (Eph. 6 : 21), "minister Dei" (II Cor. 6 : 4), etc.; in French, *ministre*, in English "minister."

creature who is suffering from evil, from sin. "C'est, non Damoclès, mais bien sa maladie qui l'intéresse" (328), the *garçon* comments, reporting Zeus's attitude of scientific detachment. Gide's God is the God of the Romantics, who con-
demns because he has made man's moral life impossible ("la
moralité privée" par Dieu!). Zeus is touched neither by Coclès's anxiety nor by Damoclès's agonies. Like Blake's "Nobo-
daddy," a sardonic and unmoved mover, he plays the experi-
mentalist who calmly watches the effects of his gratuitous
act. The *garçon* imitates Zeus the observer: "Si vous croyez
que tout ça le tourmente [Zeus]!! C'est comme moi: il observe . . . ." (317) "To observe" at the same time implies
for Zeus the observance of his own laws for predestination
and grace, and for the *garçon* that of the rites of his cult. In
an interview, Zeus reveals his protean nature to the "observing" and "observant" *garçon*. He first appears as the occult
force of finance capital—the *Prométhée*'s action falls into
the period of the Dreyfus affair, and Gide seems to avail himself of an opportunity to express his discretely *Dreyfusard*
attitude, deriding the *anti-Dreyfusards*' professed fear of a
conspiracy of "international Jewish finance capital." "Vous
me croyez banquier; je suis bien autre chose," Zeus tells the
garçon. "Mon action . . . est cachée, mais n'est pas moins con-
sidérable" (329). But he immediately changes into the Leib-
nizian watchmaker God: "Oui, j'ai surtout l'esprit d'initia-
tive. Je lance. Puis, une fois une affaire lancée, je la laisse;
je n'y touche plus" (329). He distributes those eagles which,
as conscience and consciousness, devour all vitality. He himself has no eagle. "Pas plus que dans le creux de la main,"
he asserts (330), alluding to his omnipotence as that of a
Lord who hath measured the waters "in the hollow of his
hand" and whose Spirit has not been "directed" by any
"counsellor" (Isa. 40 : 12-13). Zeus, the *"garçon*'s friend,"
(328) is humbly told by this minister, "[On dit] que vous

êtes le Bon Dieu"; and he answers with truly Gidean co-
quetry, "Je me le suis laissé dire . . . ." (330).

Mystery and mystification: the problems of free will, predestination, and grace—or determinism. The doctrinary *garçon* as propagator of the divine Word speaks of his long
hesitation between belief and disbelief in man's freedom of
action: "J'ai longtemps pensé que c'était là ce qui distinguait
l'homme des animaux: une action gratuite" (305). The feminine form *action gratuite*, its gender implying passivity, seems
here to contrast a fallible human action with the creative
acte gratuit, the divine act of grace. "J'appelais l'homme:
l'animal capable d'une action gratuite" (305). The sentence
twists Aristotle's definition of man as an *animal rationale*,
suggesting the hubris involved in any attempt to liken man's
supposed freedom of rational action with the irrational mystery of the divine act of grace. Faced with this inscrutable
matter of faith, the *garçon* resists the temptation of determinism: "Ça n'est pas pourtant que je sois déterministe" (305) by
professing belief in the paradoxical coexistence of free will
and predestined grace. He also accepts the absurdity of a
"calling" that does not necessarily result in the "choosing"
of the elect: "Il s'agit de trouver quelqu'un sans le choisir"
(306). In these words he explains the deceptive call which
goes out to Damoclès by way of the banker's *acte gratuit*.
The fate of Gide's Damoclès resembles in fact that of his
legendary namesake at the court of the tyrant Dionysius I:
"Destrictus ensis impia / Cervice pendet" ("over whose impious head the drawn sword hangeth," Horace *Carmina*
3.1.17), or as Cicero, who tells the anecdote, comments, "Sa-
tisne videtur declarasse Dionysius nihil esse ei beatum, cui
semper aliqui terror impendeat?" ("Does not Dionysius seem
to have said plainly that there was no prosperity for a man
perpetually threatened by terror?" Cicero *Disput. tuscul.*
5.62). Just as the knowledge of the sword suspended over

his neck by a horsehair (*ibid.*) destroys the Syracusan cour-
tier's joy in his lord's gift, so Gide's Damoclès is unable to
enjoy the money sent him by Zeus: he is devoured by his
lack of faith (his particular "eagle"); his bad conscience
about the undeserved grace bestowed upon him makes of him
a desperate seeker for his creditor to whom he wants to return the five hundred franc note. It was given him to deprive
him of his peace, and for the amusement of Zeus. As in
Calvinist doctrine, the "call from without" must be com-
plemented by an "inner call" which Damoclès cannot experience. He lacks the primary condition for listening to the
potential call from within, namely faith ("The wicked man
travaileth with pain all his days. . . . A dreadful sound is in his
ears: in prosperity the destroyer shall come upon him. He
believeth not that he shall return out of darkness, and he is
waited for by the sword," Job 15 : 20-22). Zeus experiments,
playing his deceptive game at Damoclès's expense: "J'aime
qu'on ne sache pas que je prête. Je joue, mais je cache
mon jeu. J'expérimente. . . . Ce que je prête aux hommes, ce
que je plante en l'homme, je m'amuse à ce que cela pousse;
je m'amuse à le voir pousser. L'homme sans quoi serait si
vide!" (329) This passage anticipates the essence of Prometheus's parable of Tityre and his tree. Efficient grace is without us and can enter into us only through faith. Not the
means of grace, not faith, not freedom, not redemption are
planted here, but servitude, suffering, malicious joy at the
damnation of others. "Je suis descendu dans la rue," Zeus explains his intentions, "cherchant le moyen de faire souffrir
quelqu'un du don que j'allais faire à quelque autre; de faire
jouir cet autre du mal que j'allais faire à cet un": for Coclès
the slap in the face (which he hardly feels at all); for Damoclès the five hundred francs, a carte blanche of pardon which
painfully weighs on his conscience as a debt heavier to bear
than the sins it is supposed to wipe out. The means of grace

are clearly perceptible; the principle of their distribution,
"la façon de les donner" (329) remains unclear and unintelligible. Prometheus, who has every reason to believe that
he knows this principle, is grouchily put into his place by
Zeus with a crude "Et quoi! vous connaissez" (329). Zeus
wants to keep his prestige: prestige not only literally but in
the primitive sense of the word (still current in the age of
the Reformation), i.e., a sorcery, an illusion, a deception, a
magician's trick ("Je ne veux pas perdre mon prestige," 333),
a major reason why he does not make himself known to
Damoclès. The secret of the illusion must be kept to the
bitter end, and possibly beyond. Hence too the *acte gratuit*
does not make apparent precisely who is redeemed, in whose
person, under whose mask. Is it the Cyclops-like Coclès, the
"natural" man (310), who gives his eye for an eye (of glass)
which he wears "not without grace" (*pas sans grâce,* 316),
a man of faith, gratitude, and works? Coclès who (in vain) offers the other cheek (Luke 6 : 29)—"il tend en vain son
autre joue" (328)—and cautiously seeks and "researches"
Zeus, only to avoid him, without knowing why, and without
ever seeing him again ("je recherchai bien mon giffleur; oui,
mais ce fut pour l'éviter, . . . et si je l'évitai, ce fut sans le
savoir," 311f.)? (The *passé simple* indicates the uniqueness
of this search and research which took place once, in the
past.) In short, is Coclès redeemed by the sacrifice of Damoclès the Jansenist or Calvinist pessimist who, graceless, *in-
grate,* simply cannot believe in "sufficient grace"? Or is Damoclès saved despite his ungracious ingratitude and his sickness
unto death, healed after death because of Zeus's *acte gratuit,*
his capricious and disturbingly ambiguous gift of grace? Does
Damoclès's fleshly death precede his spiritual rebirth? Impenetrable, the "banker's" *acte gratuit* illustrates the mystery
of Christ's deputyship, the interchangeability of guilt and ex-
piation (II Cor. 5 : 18-21), and Joseph de Maistre's doctrine of

the reversibility of guilt and punishment, according to which
in the plan of divine love the seemingly guiltless are made to
suffer and expiate for the guilty. From the divine viewpoint,
sub aeternitatis specie, the question of who suffers for whom is
indifferent. All of Zeus's experiments are admissible since original sin has affected all mankind with collective guilt. "Car
parce que l'acte est gratuit, il est ce que nous appelons ici:
réversible," explains the *garçon:* "Un qui a reçu cinq cents
francs pour un soufflet, l'autre qui a reçu un soufflet pour cinq
cents francs" (306). This grotesque commentary in the circus
style of clowneries underlines the indifference—i.e., the *equiv-
alence*—of reward and punishment: there is nothing to choose
between Coclès and Damoclès, *l'un vaut l'autre.* The *garçon's* pious gloss stresses the one-sidedness of free grace (*gratia gratis data*). Zeus may give or lend as much as he likes;
the recipient of his unwanted gifts or loans, however, is not
allowed to refuse or return his gracious grants. Coclès, in the
spirit of Jansenism and the Reformation, is drastically taught
the Pauline doctrine that without deserving it he is "justified
freely by his [God's] grace through the redemption that is
in Christ Jesus" (Rom. 3 : 24). Neither participation in the
sacraments nor good works can be of assistance; free grace
alone, *l'acte gratuit,* is efficient; and free grace, at first glance,
does not seem to be bestowed upon Coclès. Free grace is
radically opposed to salvation through the obedient observance of the law (Rom. 5 : 21; 6 : 14; Gal. 5 : 4). It precludes
in Paul's teachings the very tokens of obedience to the law:
good works (Coclès's eagerness in the prelude, his establishment of a hospital for the one-eyed) and "fleshly wisdom"
(II Cor. 1 : 12), i.e., Coclès's natural goodness. But the redemption of Damoclès too remains dubious, in spite of his
calling: he failed to be justified by faith (Rom. 5 : 1f.).

Mystery and mystification: as soon as the *garçon* attempts
to apply reasoning to the complex problems of this situation,

all categories become tangled. The incomprehensible mystery of the *acte gratuit* is confused with the human rationality of the *action gratuite* (306, 329). The *garçon* gets lost in the labyrinth of the inscrutables while there emerge simultaneously the demoralizing aspects of predestination and grace which seem to render superfluous, useless, redundant all moral efforts and behaviour: "Et puis on ne sait plus . . . on s'y perd—Songez donc! une action gratuite! il n'y a rien de plus démoralisant" (306). Faced with the insoluble mystery, all "knowledge" comes to an end. Seen from the vantage point of human reason and reduced to the level of an impulsive and free action (*l'action gratuite*), the divine act of grace appears to be little more than a disinterested yet absurd game, a sort of first prize won in the lottery of providence (329)—a winning ticket for which the winner did not pay, which won *sans raison* and, taken at face value, does not seem to benefit the winner; altogether a puzzling happening, totally devoid of morality (*la moralité privée!*), profitless, a game for game's sake to which Zeus alone holds all the clues. "Moi seul, celui-là seul dont la fortune est *infinie* peut agir avec un désintéressement absolu; l'homme pas. De là vient mon amour du jeu; non pas du gain, comprenez-moi—du jeu; que pourrais-je gagner que je n'aie pas d'avance? Le temps même. . . ." (329). The disinterested game with grace and predestination reveals itself as the impulsive pastime of a God who has exiled himself from time, taking refuge in eternity. The sporadic experimentation with which he passes away the time resembles a parody of the positivistic *Zeitgeist* of the 1890s, the spirit of scientific observation which overlaps that of Zola's naturalist manifesto on *Le Roman expérimental* (scorned by Gide) and where the ills of man in society are seen *à travers un tempérament*, but with a clinical detachment similar to Zeus's attitude toward the dying Damoclès. Viewed in this fashion, there seems to be a com-

mon denominator of farce and disinterested gambling—conscious on the divine level, unsuspected on that of the creature
—between *l'acte gratuit*, the capricious act of grace, and *l'action gratuite*, the free, rational, "scientifically correct" action
by which Man in search of salvation (theological, scientific,
or novelistic) is unknowingly led into a grotesque impasse.

4. Sortes Vergilianae, *or The Lottery of Predestination*

Revelation can be given through the casting of lots (Josh.
18 : 6; Acts 1 : 26). "Sortilege" is *sortes legere*, reading the
outcome of events from sacred lots, as practiced by Homer's
Greeks and by Mopsus when the Argonauts embarked. *Fatum*
is the oracular word, the word as fate, and soothsaying an
attempt to influence the course of future happenings, to
force fate into a mold. In the Virgilian lots (*sortes Vergilianae*) the future is foretold by opening at random a volume
of Virgil: Virgil the necromancer whose fourth *Eclogue* was
believed to be typological, a prophecy of Christianity; Virgil,
who was glorified in Dante's *Divina Commedia* as a prophet
of Christianity and regarded throughout the Middle Ages
and the Renaissance as *anima naturaliter Christiana*, a Christian soul by nature. The *sortes Vergilianae* are a rite piously
performed by medieval Christians. A prophecy is captured
by pricking a needle into the haphazardly opened New Testament or the Virgilian codex. The word caught, in more than
one sense a "catchword," foretells and influences the future.
Augustine called this type of white magic *de paginis evangelicis sortes legere* ("soothsaying from the pages of the Gospels," *Ep.* 119). As literal interpretation of biblical passages,
sortes Vergilianae are a sortilege practiced to the present day
by fundamentalists.

The lots of Damoclès and Coclès—their respective conscience and consciousness, their "eagles"—are determined by the casting of lots, by a divine "coup de dés [qui] jamais n'abolira le hasard." Damoclès "called" dies while doubting his potential redemption. Coclès, "fallen" under a divine blow and deprived of an eye by a blow of the divine eagle's wing, Coclès, severely tried by Zeus, survives and participates with Prometheus and the *garçon* in the banquet of life: the divine casting of the dice has not abolished chance.

The lots of Damoclès and Coclès picked by a needle in God's creative Word are objects, played into their hands by Zeus as matters of chance: for Coclès the *mouchoir*, the sudarium; for Damoclès the five hundred franc note. The sudarium might be that of Lazarus risen from the dead (John 11 : 44), a dark prophecy of salvation for Coclès ("Non est ad astra mollis a terris via"; "Does not the road to heaven lead through new-turned earth?" Seneca *Herc. fur.* 437). Or it might be the sudarium of the wicked servant, who hoards in it his master's pound without accumulating interest. It is taken away from its idle keeper, "For I say unto you, That unto every one which hath shall be given; and from him that hath not, even that he hath shall be taken away from him" (Luke 19 : 11-26); or, Matthew 25 : 27, "il te fallait donc remettre mon argent aux banquiers." A prophecy of Coclès's damnation and Damoclès's redemption? God's word picked by lot for Damoclès? In the parable of the two debtors (Luke 7 : 41), one owes "five hundred pence," and the other fifty; "And when they had nothing to pay, he frankly forgave them both" (Luke 7 : 42). Coclès and Damoclès likewise have nothing to pay, for everything belongs to the "Miglionnaire," to Zeus who allows himself to be called "le Bon Dieu" and who can frankly forgive his debtors by free grace, *l'acte gratuit.* "Nullus enim potest per seipsum a debito peccati liberari, nisi divina gratia veniam consequatur"; "No one can be freed from the debt of sins, unless divine grace will follow mercy" (Pope Gregory the Great, *XXXIIIa*

Homelia in evang).[7] The moral: the debtor whom the creditor loves most is the one whom he has forgiven most (Luke
7 : 42-43), provided, of course, that the borrower show "gratitude." This latter grace depends on his knowledge of his
master's forgiveness. Zeus, worried about his "prestige," does
not let himself be loved. Damoclès is allowed to feel his
"guilt," the burden of his fated and fateful "debt," but he will
never know his creditor's name; his life-destroying doubts
prevent *fides* (both "faith," and, in its Latin meaning, "monetary credit"). Lacking faith and *gratia praeveniens* ("antici-
patory grace" which enlightens understanding), he cannot
believe in forgiveness of his "debt." He is unable to curb his
impious curiosity to know a creditor who wants to remain
incognito, *Deus ignotus*, the unknown God. Grace is with-
held from him; he cannot be grateful for a "debt" which
he had no desire to contract. Hence he lacks the two primary
conditions for "forgiveness": faith and the inner grace of
gratitude. His "humiliation," quite literally a "lowering"
(conveyed by way of a medical image, *un rétrécissement de
la colonne,"* 328) occurs after Prometheus's speech exhorting
all men to love their devouring eagles in order to ensure the
beauty of these birds of prey (327). Damoclès's irredeemable
ills increase while Coclès (for whom he worries) painfully
attempts to sacrifice himself: "Il [Coclès] ne parle plus que
de se dévouer et passe tout son temps à chercher partout
dans les rues une nouvelle gifle qui vaille quelque argent
à quelque nouveau Damoclès. Il tend en vain l'autre joue"
(328). The *garçon* suggests to Prometheus that only a
"brusque and miraculous salvation" (328) could help Damoclès: "A moins d'un salut brusque et miraculeux, le mal ne
peut que s'aggraver. Il est très bas, je vous assure" (328)—
an ambiguous hint at Damoclès's "humiliation" in the scrip-

---

[7] Quoted by Thomas Aquinas as a gloss to Luke 7 : 42-43 in *Catena
aurea* (Venice, 1746), II, 127.

tural sense of the word. The creditor avoids any contact with
Damoclès and even with Coclès, to whom he had shown
himself once. For Damoclès he remains *deus absconditus*,
the hidden God, never manifesting himself as *deus revelatus*,
the revealed God, in the spirit of *gemina praedestinatio*,
twin predestination, as Augustine, Luther, and Calvin (*Institutio* III, ch. 21ff.) had taught. For both Coclès and Damoclès, this hidden God without revelation has staged an eschatological joke without apocalyptic significance. In a Calvinist
sense, Damoclès cannot believe in grace offered him without
revelation; nor can Coclès by his eager devotion, by "passing
all his time in the streets looking for a new slap" (328), find
that "free grace" which "is not of him that willeth nor of
him that runneth, but of God that showeth mercy" (Rom.
9 : 16). Damoclès lacks *gratia efficax*, efficient grace which
alone can enlighten, Augustine's *crede ut intelligas* ("believe"
—but also in an economic sense, "lend," "loan"—"so that
you may understand"). Where there is no efficient grace,
there can be no answer to questions even if the questioning
follows the best scholastic order of *cur, unde, quo, qua* (309).
"Votre gain prenait sur ma misère," Coclès reproaches Damoclès (312). But the treasure which, thanks to Coclès's suffering, fell into Damoclès's lap oppresses Damoclès; he is tor-
mented at the idea that "c'est grâce à la gifle d'un autre que
je tiens là ces cinq cents francs!" (331) These undeserved
riches are useless to him but he is incapable of parting with
them. He does not dare to consider them as a "reward," a
salary earned for his salvation (*salus* meaning health). Con-
sequently he does not deposit this money in "the savings
bank" (*la Caisse d'épargne*, 331) as savings which bring interest (*œconomia*, in the patristic vocabulary of salvation).
The result is that altogether the worries about his "debt,"
the unrestituted five hundred francs, poison his life. They
are his Promethean eagle, his "idiosyncrasy"; inalienably

rooted in his conscience and consciousness, they keep him out of the kingdom of heaven ("Verily I say unto you, That a rich man shall hardly enter into the kingdom of heaven" [Matt. 19 : 23]). Neither for Coclès nor for Damoclès do the prophecies of the *sortes Vergilianae* abolish chance. Instead of bringing health and freedom (*franchise, affranchissement*) to Damoclès, the "hated, execrated" five hundred francs seem to enslave him toward everyman, toward all and no one in particular: "Ces cinq cents francs, haïs, exécrés, je croyais les devoir à tous et n'osais les donner à aucun—j'en aurais *privé tous les autres*" (331). The impasse of charity and grace (χάρις) is one of choice and cruelty, the privilege of the powerful, the mystery of the Almighty, inaccessible to Damoclès whose moral scruples keep him within that limbo of indecision where dwell *le genti dolorose / C'hanno perduto il ben dell'intelletto* ("the suffering race / Who have lost the wealth of intellect," Dante, *Inferno* III, 17-18). Once each week he brings the worthless means of grace back into circulation without being able to cast it off: he changes the banknote into coins, the coins again into a banknote. "C'est une folie circulaire" (331), the vicious circle of an ever-repeated exchange without redemption that encompasses and stifles his life; the whole process is economically unsound, and does not lead to salvation. The moral dilemma produced by Zeus's immoral gift of grace ruins his health; the interplay of Damoclès's lack of merit, his feelings of indebtedness and duty (*dettes* and *devoir*), as well as the concealed and impenetrable identity of his creditor and "benefactor," undermine his vital substance: "Seigneur! Seigneur!" he cries out, "à qui devais-je? . . . Le devoir, Messieurs, c'est une chose horrible; moi, j'ai pris le parti d'en mourir" (331f.). The guilt feeling that drives him freely to choose death deprives him of free actions (*les actions gratuites*). He is literally possessed by his "possession," the obsessive five hundred francs which weigh on him so that he cannot be supernaturally uplifted by *gratia elevans,* uplifting grace. "Denarios quingentos," five hundred francs, those *fata* (oracular and fatal words) determining his lot, also point to the fact that redemption was lost on the "boulevard qui mène de la Madeleine à l'Opéra" (Coclès's broad road of Damascus, leading from sin to operative grace) where the passing crowd (*massa perditionis,* "the masses of the damned"—but also "the bankrupt"!) in vain seek their salvation, their personalities, their idiosyncrasies (304), and where Coclès had earned for his good deed the brutal reprobation of Zeus. The grateful sinner who in the house of Simon the Pharisee had washed with her tears and anointed Christ's feet (Luke 7 : 36ff.) is traditionally confused with Mary Magdalene ("la Madeleine"). "Therefore I tell you that her sins, her many sins, must have been forgiven her, or she would not have shown such great love" (Luke 7 : 47). "Your faith has saved you" (Luke 7 : 50). In the medicoeconomic vocabulary of salvation faith and love have saved and enriched the sinner. They are precisely those gifts of grace which Damoclès lacks in order to be healed and freed of his debts; their absence drives him to his death.

5. Guilt, Debts, Duty

In their eagerness to fulfill the law, their *devoir,* and to follow the voice of reason, Coclès and Damoclès are incapable of understanding that self-humiliation and unquestioning faith are prerequisites for efficient grace. Opposed to the rationality of the law (Rom. 5 : 21; 6 : 14; Gal. 5 : 4), efficient grace precludes rewards for good works (Rom. 4 : 4; 11 : 5f.; 3 : 24) and frustrates the "fleshly wisdom" (II Cor. 1 : 12) of reasoning. Seeking their salvation on the broad road "where sin [abounds]" without knowing that "there [does] grace much more abound" (Rom. 5 : 20), they want to ob-

tain redemption by performing their duty. They remain un-
redeemed as long as they fail to comprehend the christologi-
cal miracle of redemption from the law. It is true that Damoclès, through the five hundred francs, has an epiphany, an
Easter experience of sorts; they give him his *nouvelles pensées*, uplifting him from the triviality of his *anciennes
pensées*. The old Adam seems to give way to the new man:
"Je menais une vie parfaitement ordinaire et me faisais un
devoir de cette formule: ressembler au plus commun des
hommes" (308). The observance of the law (*devoir*) is now
replaced by Damoclès's discovery of his uniqueness, a distinction bestowed upon him by Zeus's *acte gratuit* through
which Damoclès feels that he has been chosen: "Or, . . .
depuis trente jours, je sens que je suis un être original, unique,
répondant à une singulière destinée" (308). Thirty days of
the new and unique life, the new month or moon (*lune*)
of a singular destiny, of spiritual rebirth in an idiosyncrasy
at last found, stand in a cryptic relationship to Prometheus's
discourse in the *salle des nouvelles lunes* (320-327), that sort
of auditorium and hall of a new age, a new aeon where the
revelation of the Incarnate Word ("le Discours de Prométhée") appears to cause Damoclès's fatal disease and Coclès's
conspicuous restoration to health: "Le secret de leur vie est
dans le dévouement à leur dette; toi, Coclès, à ta gifle; toi,
Damoclès, à ton billet" (327). Damoclès fails to understand
Prometheus's warning: "[il te fallait] garder tes cinq cents
francs, continuer de les devoir sans honte, d'en devoir plus
encore, de devoir avec joie" (327). Damoclès's fears, his
life-devouring conscience, his joyless ingratitude for the free
gift of a new personality, an idiosyncrasy, demonstrate his
inability to recognize the signs of grace mysteriously bestowed
on his person which could not have been attained by external means (*ex opere operato*, "by grace worked through
the sacrament"). By refusing his lot in the lottery of grace,

he throws away his life. He cannot redeem the five hundred
francs which he does not allow to redeem him. Without
blind acceptance and love of his fate (the Nietzschean *amor
fati*), the sortilege cast upon him by his fate must needs become fatal to him. For he tries to rid himself of that which
the passersby in vain attempt to find on the sinful road of
the law, the "boulevard qui mène de la Madeleine à l'Opéra."
Neither the unexpected letter with the five hundred francs
nor Prometheus's discourse is interpreted by Damoclès as
the revelation of his redemption: both give him the painful
awareness of a debt unwittingly contracted and for which
nonetheless he must assume full responsibility. Zeus's gift of
grace, freely played into his hands by the stupidity of chance,
ignites in him a fervor not of belief but of desperate longing
for some sign of life from his creditor.

6. *Letter against Spirit*

Zeus's letter to Damoclès contains the five hundred franc
note, a material gift (or loan) but no spiritual message. Not
knowing what to make of it, Damoclès takes the envelope
with its address "d'une écriture inconnue" (309)—*écriture*
meaning "handwriting," but also "scripture"—to a number
of graphologists for a minute analysis. In these graphologists
one easily recognizes a modern metaphor for the Sopherim,
the Biblical scribes, learned in the Scriptures and in the exposition of the law, but always presented in the New Testament as myopic jurists deeply concerned with the letter of
the law, blind and deaf to the spirit, and devoid of any understanding for the mysteries of grace. The spirit of this
écriture, this Scripture, remains unknown to the scribes as
well as to Damoclès. According to the judgment of some
graphologists, it testified to the great bounty (*d'une grande
bonté*) on the part of the writer; others saw in it signs of

weakness (*plutôt de la faiblesse,* 309). Damoclès concludes: "Le manque complet de caractère qu'elle [l'écriture] m'a révélé dans la suite par l'entremise des graphologues consultés ne m'a permis de rien apprendre" (309). The writer, of course, was Coclès; his "manque complet de caractère" points to the absence of a personality, of an "idiosyncrasy" of his own. As writer of the unknown scripture, the *écriture inconnue* addressed to Damoclès which so badly upsets the latter, he seems to reveal a second identity: that of a scriptural writer of epistles containing a message of grace, incomprehensible to human reason. In other words, Coclès is at the same time the "old Adam" (Saul) and the "new man" (Paul); his encounter with Zeus on the *grands boulevards* represented Saul's conversion into Paul on the road to Damascus as well as Adam's fall. His persecution of the Lord turned into the pursuit of the Lord: in the grotesque language of the *sotie,* the handkerchief dropped (and picked up) as a coquettish token of erotic intentions ("love") and the blow given to Coclès represent Saul's fall and subsequent rise on the way to Damascus, his rebirth as Paul which makes him oblivious to the suffering inflicted upon him by Zeus, the threefold God (Zeus, the Father; the banker, $\sigma\omega\tau\acute{\eta}\rho$, the savior; the "Miglionnaire," the Holy Spirit—cast out to the millions of believers as the promised riches of the millennium).

By having the mere envelope of Zeus's gift analysed by dubious graphologists, Damoclès proceeds like the scribes of the new Testament, but also like Protestant exegetes and textual critics whose rationalist literal-mindedness enables them to realize the human origins of the *écriture,* the scriptural manuscript (the "bounty" or "weakness" of Coclès–Saul–Paul). What they all fail to see is its spirit, the symbolism of the mystery, Zeus's *acte gratuit* which, in the form of the trivial five hundred franc note, was concealed underneath the human handwriting—mysterious in itself and hidden in its envelope—in vain awaiting Damoclès's confession of faith, which alone could have activated its liberating gift of grace. But Damoclès is not redeemed, for he follows Coclès in his footsteps on the road to Damascus without understanding the sign which is sent him. He only knows of his guilt, and this rational knowledge of his debt causes him to fulfill his *devoir*, to live up to the demands of the law by the use of external means of grace (*ex opere operato*, on the way to the Opéra): "Reconnaissant, je voudrais l'être—mais je ne sais pas envers qui" (309). He feels enslaved to Zeus's banknote, not realizing that it is his free ticket, his pass for redemption: "Avant j'étais banal mais libre. A présent j'appartiens à lui [billet]" (310). Shortsightedly he cannot see beyond the present moment. Damoclès's unrecognized passport for salvation turns into chagrin, shagreen, a Balzacian *peau de chagrin*, a property of which the owner cannot rid himself and which rapidly shortens his life.[8] Coclès too refuses the gift of grace for purely legal reasons; he is careful not to pass on Zeus's slap to Damoclès—preventing him from having a "road to Damascus" experience—for he fears "Si je vous avais rendu la gifle vous eussiez cru devoir me rendre ce billet, et . . . il ne m'appartient pas" (310). Having only written the address on the envelope, he remains in the dark and fearful as to the meaning of its contents.

The chance of predestination determines the receiver of the fateful gift of grace. Coclès fortuitously (*fortuitement*, 310) knew Damoclès by his name, by a strange hazard which however approached a mysterious and mystifying illumination: "Le nom que j'inscrivis, et qui vint je ne sais comment dans ma tête, était pour moi celui d'un inconnu!" (311)

[8] It brings to mind Hercules's sacrifice for Prometheus, as a result of which he died (a typological Christ figure), maddened by Deianeira's gift of the Nessus shirt.

Arbitrarily, Coclès had become the instrument of revelation
(in his own way, a myopic "scribe" of providence to whom
the spirit of the "letter" he inscribed remained unknown).
Arbitrarily, Damoclès had misunderstood the meaning of this
revelation. He had seen his only salvation in the remote possibility of redeeming his mysterious and unrecognized pass
to redemption by returning it to his unknown creditor. Obviously, Zeus's offer of grace had not been a serious one, for
predestination refused Damoclès the receiving grace of faith
without which he could not have received salvation. Finally,
chance had determined the fall of Coclès as the punishment
and reward of someone who has persecuted, and (without
knowing it) pursued, sought the Lord and seen the hidden
God, *Deus absconditus*: Coclès, the receiver of the burning
blow dealt him by a god (311), of the Promethean fire, of
ardent illumination, and of Gidean *ferveur*—Coclès–Saul–
Paul on the road to Damascus; and Coclès, the narrow-
minded, who loses one eye to the Promethean eagle, to the
descending Holy Spirit—Coclès–Paul, the myopic Pauline
tradition (as seen by Gide), one-eyed in its lacking of depth-
perception. Limited, and full of good will, Coclès is always
ready for external grace: "Mon désir n'étant point de me
soustraire à une motivation extérieure, je me soumis" (311).
For a Christian, his behavior is at least externally correct. He
begins his *histoire* with repeated assertions that he has no
great relations on earth: "Je n'ai pas grandes relations sur
la terre" (310, 311). He proves his missionary zeal, his piety
(328). As the founder of a hospital for the one-eyed (a refuge
for those suffering from literal-mindedness) he shows his
charity (317); and he even follows the command of the
Sermon on the Mount by offering (however vainly) his other
cheek (328). But everything points to the fact that Coclès–
Saul–Paul remains until Damoclès's death a figure not of the
present but of the Mosaic law, even of Moses himself: his

face's burning from Zeus's slap gives witness to his vision of
God; what Coclès brings back is the law and the Messianic
promise. Even in the hospital which he directs, the one-eyed
inmates seem to owe their condition to the survival of the
"old law" of "an eye for an eye." And the *garçon*, with Christian anti-Semitism, accuses Coclès of being crafty in his
business dealings: "C'est un roublard. Avec l'argent que lui
rapporte la collecte, il songe à fonder un hospice. . . . Un
petit, oui; rien que pour les borgnes. Il s'en est nommé di-
recteur" (317). As the Church was founded with secular
means, and upon the doctrines of Paul, so, in a Nietzschean
sense, he founds a hospital for those who are failing, shady,
suspicious (*borgnes!*), kings among the blind. In sum, nothing has changed since the days of the law, nothing will change
until the death of Damoclès and the protean Coclès's redemption from the shackles of Pauline teachings at the banquet of life where, in the company of the *garçon* and Prometheus, the Promethean eagle is eaten.

Two. ON THE SEESAW OF TWIN PREDESTINATION

1. *The Ups and Downs of Spiritual Brotherhood*

THE DICHOTOMY of "Histoire de Coclès," "Histoire de Damoclès," represents two blundering attitudes of the faithful throughout the history of Christianity. Inseparably linked by Providence, Coclès and Damoclès play the *sotie* of the two equally impenetrable aims, the mysterious ends of predestination according to Augustine and Calvin: election and preterition. Ambiguous is the choice of either man, ambiguous his potential rejection. Both seem to be chosen and doomed by turns, and again chosen after their doom, *gratuitement, fortuitement, providentiellement* (331), in accordance with Matt. 19 : 30: "But many that are first shall be last; and the last shall be first." There only appears to be some doubt as to who is among the first, who among the last, Coclès or Damoclès. It is the supralapsarian comedy of errors. Coclès, who has *le naturel bon*, is slapped by Zeus and insufficiently (if at all) enlightened by his "road to Damascus" experience; Damoclès, favored by external grace, must look with suspicion upon his good fortune and perish through it, with dubious hopes of redemption. On the seesaw of *gemina praedestinatio*, twin predestination, Coclès is struck to the ground, while Damoclès is lifted up; when Damoclès lies on his deathbed, Coclès finds the full enjoyment of his health. In the spirit of Christian brotherhood, both are worried about one another but mainly about the other's guilt, weakness, and failings, mistaking the other's suffering for a blissful gain. As Coclès puts it: "Entre votre gain et ma peine il y a une relation;

63

je ne sais pas laquelle—mais il y a une relation" (312). The "je ne sais pas laquelle" piously acknowledges the mystery of this "relation," a word describing a relationship of members of one body, but also starkly hinting at an account, a report (relation) on this mystery to be read between the lines of "Histoire de Coclès" and "Histoire de Damoclès." Coclès and Damoclès are two members of one body, connected to the very end by their alternate calls and reprovals. The *garçon*, the minister, explains his own function as that of a connecting link: ". . . j'écoute, je relate; eux subissent la relation . . . mon goût à moi, c'est de créer des relations. . . ." (305). He establishes the rapport among Coclès, Damoclès, and Prometheus, who has come down from the heights of the Caucasus as the prescient Logos, the real presence of the Incarnate Word. Coclès, Damoclès, and Prometheus, served by the *garçon*, represent the Church as the body of Christ with its members and head: "For as the body is one, and hath many members, and all the members of that one body, being many, are one body: so also is Christ. For by one Spirit are we all baptized into one body, whether we be Jews or Gentiles, whether we be bond or free; and have been all made to drink into one Spirit" (I Cor. 12 : 12-13). Coclès, Damoclès, and Prometheus "drink into one Spirit" under the *garçon's* ministration, communing and communicating in the café, where the *coitus electorum (reprobatorumque)* of Augustine and Calvin, the community of the chosen and the reproved, have intercourse, illustrating the unique and impenetrable principle of predestined election. Behind the scene, Zeus determines the course of the divine game of blindman's buff (or of providence) with the members of the mystical body, *corpus mysticum*, of the congregation gathered in Ecclesia (the café), the Eucharist (their symbolic meal, see below [305, 307]) and Evangelium, the Good Word: a fulfillment unknown to Damoclès of his ardent

wish, "ressembler au plus commun des hommes" (308)—
blending into κοινωνία, the community which is *communica-
tio* (communication and communion) (I Cor. 10 : 16),
where suddenly, and without motivation, the lot of redemption or damnation is played into the hands of the faithful.

Ecclesia, the Church, the restaurant on the "boulevard
qui mène de la Madeleine à l'Opéra": here Prometheus in-
differently awaits the clients, while the *garçon* gives him an
account of the particular rites which are performed in his
establishment. To restore oneself, one sits *par tables de trois*
(305) facing a sort of chalice (*un bock*) in close communication (*on cause*, 305): it is *communio sub utraque specie*—
communion under both species—the Protestant sacrament
with the chalice also for the layman. The new covenant
("For this is my blood, the blood of the new covenant,"
Matt. 26 : 28) is mediated by the *garçon*. "Trois messieurs
arrivent; on les présente (quand ils le demandent, naturellement)" (305). There follows the dual presence and presentation of the Trinity (in the person of Prometheus, the savior
of mankind, descended from above) and the community
(Coclès, Damoclès) and, "in the midst of them," Prometheus: "For where two or three are gathered together in my
name, there am I in the midst of them" (Matt. 18 : 20).
"Parce qu'à mon restaurant, avant le dîner," (before the reenactment of the Last Supper) "on doit dire son nom; et
puis ce qu'on fait; tant pis si on se trompe." Baptism ("on
doit dire son nom"), an expression of the presence of the
Lord in "His name" (Acts 3 : 16; 4 : 12, etc.) as well as a
confession of faith, the creed, and true faith itself, self-knowledge founded upon the knowledge of God (Calvin, *Institutio*
I, 1), must have preceded Holy Communion, for without
true faith (according to Luther and Calvin) this sacrament
could only harm the participant. "Alors on s'assied (pas
moi)"—the seated congregation, the standing minister—"on

cause (pas moi non plus)—mais je mets en relation; j'écoute; je scrute; je dirige la conversation" (305). Minister and congregation listen to the Holy Ghost that only comes in the Word; the congregation makes public confession and acts of contrition; the minister explores the revealed Word and directs the service, mediating communication and Communion. "A la fin du dîner je connais trois êtres intimes, trois personnalités" (305): knowledge of the Trinity is gained through Holy Communion. The service yields no benefits to the *garçon*: "Qu'est-ce que tout cela me rapporte? Oh! rien du tout" (305). It is purely a matter of taste: "Mon goût à moi, c'est de créer des relations." Neither the community nor the minister are automatically justified by their observance of the sacraments, although the latter may strengthen, restore them. Nor can the Reformed minister absolve his coreligionists. No sacramental means of grace can influence the work of predestination; its choices were made from all eternity. Hence the divine service, as the *garçon* explains it, is "une action absolument gratuite" (305), meaning—even if no pun is intended (*absolument*, "by way of absolution")—a totally indifferent action, an absurdity, a foolish performance in the spirit of the *sotie*. The paradox of mutual accusations and callous protestations of neighborly love in the relationship between Coclès and Damoclès is equally eccentric and grotesque; their scurrilous exchanges of reproaches and names of endearment ("Cocle," "Damocle," 312 *passim*) underscore the expression of deep suspicions with regard to human nature that is rooted in Calvinist pessimism. Their "disagreeably personal conversation," full of innuendos, causes the *garçon* to divert everyone's attention to Prometheus: "Par une habile manœuvre—simplement en renversant une assiette pleine sur Prométhée, il [garçon] détourna vers celui-ci l'attention brusque des deux autres" (312). His farcical maneuver has a symbolic meaning: it figuratively identifies the food with Prometheus, the invited Lord, sacrifice (*hostia*, "the host") and guest (*hostis*). The Incarnate Word cannot suppress an exclamation which he utters in an unusually profound tone of voice ("From the depths I call to Thee, o Lord," Ps. 129). The others suddenly realize that hitherto he had remained silent. Coclès and Damoclès, thoroughly irritated, reproach him: "Mais vous ne dites rien" (312). Now Prometheus begins to speak ("Prométhée parle," 313) but what he has to say, in his own words, "a si peu de rapport" (313). Living in eternity he seems to be out of touch with the secular world of time: "Vous avez chacun votre histoire; je n'en ai pas" (313). The possibilities of communication are so weak that both Coclès and Damoclès have misgivings about his apparently futile presence. They both ask in unison: "Pourquoi êtes-vous venu ici, cher Monsieur . . . Monsieur?" (313) Prometheus is addressed as "Monsieur"— a mere title of politeness derived via *sieur* from *seigneur*, Lord. He vaguely reminds Coclès and Damoclès of a mythical person, known by hearsay; but he remains a stranger, *hostis*, and as such threatening, inimical, suspect.

2. Historical and Extrahistorical Existence

Opposite the headings "Histoire du garçon et du Miglionnaire" (304ff.), "Histoire de Damoclès" (308ff.), "Histoire de Coclès" (310ff.), "Histoire de l'aigle" (314f.) are "Prométhée parle" (313f.) and the continuation of Prometheus's discourse in the *salle des nouvelles lunes* (322ff.), as well as its conclusion (326f.). All protagonists are historical with the exception of Prometheus. Even Zeus, called "le Bon Dieu," has entered history as a mask for the God of wrath of the Old Testament. Only the Incarnate Word ("Prométhée parle") is eternal and omnipresent. Preexisting throughout eternity, Prometheus had neither known his eagle (322) nor seen him

before his theft of the divine fire which was to give both Coclès and Damoclès a sort of Gidean *ferveur* in reverse, setting
in motion the grotesque universe of the *Prométhée*. Like his
discourse, Prometheus's theft of fire, his gift to mankind, and
his sacrifice are not to be taken as historical events, occurring
in time, but as seasonal mysteries always renewing themselves,
in the spirit of John 6 (*passim*), so dear to Gide. The eagle too
belongs to history. It came and comes again at those points
of the cycle where Prometheus briefly broke and again breaks
into the realm of history to bring fire, *ferveur*, to man and to
redeem him. "Avant lui [l'aigle] j'étais inconscient et beau,
heureux et nu sans le savoir" (323). Before the eagle, Prometheus enjoyed and will enjoy again the paradisiac state of innocence; whenever the eagle came and returns, the Son of
God becomes the Son of Man. With the glorification of the
eagle (as conscience and consciousness) there begins the
eschatological striving for the historicity of Prometheus: the
attempt to tear him from eternity in order to incorporate him
in time, in history. At the rate at which his extrahistorical
freedom is endangered, his health, his eternal vitality dimin-
ishes—conditions which manifest themselves during his paradoxical detention (*prison préventive*).

According to the Calvinist view of the Eucharist, the *garçon* invites Prometheus "maintenant, si Monsieur veut bien
rentrer dans la salle; je ne peux pas servir dehors" (307).
Holy Communion cannot take place on the sinful road
(Madeleine–Opéra) outside the Church, outside the loving
community of Saints, the *coitus sanctorum*, and, least of all,
without the Lord's personal presence. "Et il [garçon] cria:—
une table de trois! une! . . ." (307). The sacrificial table
(*mensa*) is prepared, (*missa* meaning the sacrifice of the
mass, the Eucharist), in the presence of the Trinity at the
altar. As though they were "called" (I Cor. 1 : 24), two
gentlemen enter through two different doors: Coclès, "by

nature good" but fallen, originally the Jew of the Old Covenant, Saul, having become Paul after his striking experience of the New Covenant; and Damoclès, the Syracusan
Greek, the Gentile, who is offered the free pass to salvation
and the New Testament. They give their names and sit down
without asking for an introduction (307). They do not really
know one another, even if in the prologue, during his encounter on the road to Damascus, Coclès had mysteriously
known the gentile's name and obtained the gift of grace for
him, without actually being aware of what he was doing.
Although Coclès and Damoclès are "members of one body,"
their association is far from intimate; it is even uneasy. Their
failure to ask for an introduction betrays an indifference and
suspicions analogous to those prevalent among the Jewish and
Greek communicants of the early Christian Church, a lack of
communication which seemed to persist in spite of Paul's
unabated attempts to reconcile the two groups (Acts 18 : 4;
Rom. 1 : 16, 10 : 12; I Cor. 12 : 13; Gal. 3 : 28, etc.). Coclès
repeatedly observes that the food is not particularly good in
this restaurant—"attendu qu'on y mange fort mal" (307),
obviously a dual allusion to the unwillingness of the Gentiles
to observe Jewish dietary laws, and to the indifference of a
Communion which is but a token of grace, not necessarily a
means of obtaining grace, of justifying the communicant.
Here the soul only finds symbolic food without true *manducatio oralis*, without actually eating the body of Christ (a
ritual which produces no transsubstantiation) in the sense of
Augustine's "Non quod videtur, sed quod creditur pascit," in
the reenactment of the Last Supper which nourishes not
what is seen but what is believed. It is a totally abstract supper, and hence for Coclès an extremely bad one. It consists
of the simple belief in having eaten something: "Believe, and
you have eaten" (*crede, et manducasti*). In sum, the nutri-
tive value of this meal is composed of the ingredients which

the believer's faith contributes to it. The presence of the Word as interpreter and distributor is more important than the foodstuff itself: in Augustine's words, "accedit verbum ad elementum et fit sacramentum" ("the word approaches the element and makes the sacrament," i.e., produces faith). Therefore the *Verbum visibile* is invited to interpret. "Ce restaurant invite à la parole," explains the *garçon*, inviting Prometheus to reveal his *trait distinctif*. "Qu'avez-vous que n'a personne autre? *Pourquoi vous appelle-t-on Prométhée?*" The omission of *de* (*d'*) before *autre*, and the second question ("Why are you called Prescience?") indicate that the *garçon* is not asking for an explanation of Prometheus's unique properties, his attributes, but for a manifestation of his unique person, for his personal presence (313f.). The personal encounter with Prometheus leads to the revelation of his eagle, an eschatological figure, which perhaps is only a vulture (ἀετοί means both "eagles" and "vultures"): "For wherever the carcass is, there will the eagles be gathered together" (Matt. 24 : 28). Later, in the *salle des nouvelles lunes*, after much stalling and many pirouettes, the eagle lets himself be recognized as a topos for the Holy Spirit. He now coos and flutters like a dove: "L'aigle battit des ailes, roucoula" (323). Here, as elsewhere in the *Prométhée*, the definite past underscores uniqueness and presence of the legendary event which cannot become a mere routine but is for the participant a unique happening whenever he experiences it anew.

The eagle's mimetic tour de force, his performance in the role of the Holy Spirit, occurs after Prometheus has confessed that it was only for the love of Asia, his mistress, that he agreed to give up his "inhumaine solitude" (323), his preexisting state of naked beauty and innocence, so that he could "take care" of mankind (323), becoming Incarnate as the prescient Word, and making the supreme sacrifice for the love of Asia (add "Minor"), for Middle Eastern Man. First, however, Prometheus had to seek men (choose his disciples, found his ministry on earth). He found them in a piteous state: "Ils étaient très peu éclairés; j'inventai pour eux quelques feux; et dès lors commença mon aigle" (323)—the pentecostal experience of the tongues of fire, renewed by the faithful with every Holy Communion attended by belief, but also the Gidean *ferveur* accompanied by the eagle who devours his owner. The pentecostal "cloven tongues like as of fire" (Acts 2 : 3) are shown the audience by Prometheus in the form of *photographies obscènes* (321) (literally: *phos, graphos,* "writing with light," plus perhaps *ob scaena,* not to be shown on stage, since paradisiac nudity belongs to the beyond) and by the use of *"fusées volantes"* (321), which might be interpreted as figures for the Ascension bringing the light of life to the darkness of death. With the pentecostal experiences, reminiscent of the events of Easter, Prometheus's eagle begins his devouring—just as the congregation, communing in the Holy Spirit, renews the Covenant in the Eucharist, by symbolically eating and drinking the flesh and blood of the Redeemer. "Dès lors commença mon aigle. C'est depuis ce jour que je m'aperçois que je suis nu," confesses Prometheus, ambiguously suggesting his loss of innocence by his assumption of the sins of all men, and hinting at a state of total *dénuement* to which, stripped of all acquired traits and legal inheritance, the Gidean hero aspires as the end of his *attente* and *ferveur*. But things go wrong, for the narrow-minded audience interprets the message literally. Prometheus, the Christ figure cyclically devoured by his eagle, the congregation, is detained in the "body" of his community's feeble spirit (which mistakes itself for the Holy Spirit)—hence "La Détention de Prométhée." "Mange, dit Prométhée [à son aigle] en découvrant son foie" (318)—in Hesiod (*Theog.* 528), Prometheus's liver is the seat of his bitter brooding

(ἐλύσατο δυσφροσυνάων); "Take it and eat, this is my body"
(Matt. 26 : 26); "I am the bread of life" (John 6 : 48); "I
am the living bread that has come down from heaven" (John
6 : 51). The eagle, on this level of interpretation, is the abortive *corpus mysticum*, the autonomous spirit and sovereign
will of a self-righteous community that with Calvinist pessimism believes in the election of a very few, and lives in
perpetual fear of damnation instead of participating *et nunc*,
right now, in the banquet of life.

At "Pentecost," the *garçon* performs his skillful maneuver,
his diversion (a conversion) by spilling the food over Prometheus; instead of baptizing in the name of Prometheus, he
baptizes Prometheus, incorporating him into the system, as
the self-righteous spirit of the congregation pours over their
head. The *garçon's* self-righteousness causes him to perform
the "friendly service" of denouncing Prometheus, the illumi-
nator of mankind, as *fabricant d'allumettes sans brevet*, and
to bring about his arrest (315). The self-righteousness of
Coclès is manifested by his pride in his "natural bounty,"
the self-righteousness of Damoclès by his rational quest for
the creditor (*Deus ignotus*) and his intention to return the
gift of grace. The *garçon*, Coclès, and Damoclès lose the opportunity for a pentecostal experience; they fail to receive
the Holy Ghost during a Last Supper which is at the same
time a *déjeuner* (315), like Communion a breaking of the
fast, and a supper, *dîner* (305). They are presumptuous, too
full of themselves, unprepared for a spiritual rebirth, for *ferveur* and *dénuement*, and hence unfit to "eat the same spiritual meat" and to "drink the same spiritual drink" (I Cor.
10 : 3-4). The unsuccessful pentecostal mystery of "Histoire
de l'aigle" is called *votre scandale* by the *garçon* later in his
conversation with Prometheus (who then is feeding his
eagle), revealing the *scandalon*, the "stumbling block" (I
Cor. 1 : 23). It would almost seem as though Coclès were

being punished for his unseemly curiosity with regard to Prometheus's nature, and what is more, in a manner which brings to mind the story of the third one-eyed calendar in the *Arabian Nights*.[1] Gide almost literally transposes Acts 2, the tempestuous descent of the Holy Spirit: "Un oiseau qui de loin paraît énorme, mais qui n'est, vu de près, pas du tout si grand que cela, obscurcit un instant le ciel du boulevard— fond comme un tourbillon vers le café, brise la devanture, et s'abat crevant l'œil de Coclès d'un coup d'aile, et avec force pépiements tendres oui mais impérieux, s'abat sur le flanc droit de Prométhée" (314). "And when the day of Pentecost was fully come, they were all with one accord in one place"

---

[1] While composing *Le Prométhée mal enchaîné*, Gide enthusiastically read Stendhal (see his correspondence with Valéry, *passim*), and also gave stylistic advice to Dr. Mardrus, who was engaged in presenting a new translation of the *Arabian Nights*. "Je relis avec le plus grand intérêt les Mille et une Nuits de M[ardrus] et vois avec délices qu'il a tenu compte de mes quelques corrections," he wrote to Valéry on July 11, 1899; "Admirables récits des Kalenders." The reference is to the "Stories of the Three One-eyed Calenders," i.e., members of a Sufic order of wandering mendicant dervishes (the connection with Gide's Coclès, wandering in search of Zeus and begging for another slap, seems to impose itself!). These stories begin with the 37th Night. The story of the third Calender (57th Night), who loses his eye because of his restless and tactless curiosity, is of some considerable interest for Gide's treatment of Coclès. The thoroughly complicated episode is incorrectly telescoped in Stendhal's unfinished novel *Lamiel* (published posthumously in 1889). Coclès's loss of one eye seems to reflect Stendhal's summary, which confuses the Bird Roc who abducts the third Calender (57th Night) with the flying horse that knocks out his eye (62nd Night). The diabolical Dr. Sansfin suggests to the inquisitive Lamiel, eager to experiment in order to understand the secrets of love, "il y a un extrême danger pour vous à chercher de vous en éclaircir, c'est comme le secret terrible des Mille et une nuits, ces contes qui vous amusent tant: lorsque le héros veut s'en éclaircir, un énorme oiseau paraît dans le ciel qui s'abat sur lui et lui arrache un oeil" (Stendhal, *Romans et nouvelles* n.r.f., [Paris, Bibliothèque de la Pléiade], II, 947). The demonic figure of Dr. Sansfin left a profound impression on Gide; he quoted him in January 1902 (*J.* I, 108). In 1946, Gide prefaced a new edition of *Lamiel*.

(Acts 2 : 1): Coclès, Damoclès, and the administering *garçon* are all in one place with Prometheus, but not "with one accord," each one being willfully preoccupied with his own train of thought. "And suddenly there came a sound from heaven as of a rushing mighty wind, and it filled all the house where they were sitting" (Acts 2 : 2). "La rumeur dans le café fut grande" (314). "And there appeared unto them cloven tongues like of fire [*linguae tanquam ignis*]; and it sat upon each of them" (Acts 2 : 3). "J'inventai pour eux quelques feux" (323)—the *linguae tanquam ignis* which Prometheus had invented for the enlightenment of mankind, an invention which had also resulted in his eagle. The bird of prey, that "temperament" which devoured all principles, here stands for the Holy Spirit as the seat of affects and feelings (John 11 : 33) as the Lord's Spirit (II Cor. 3 : 17) that also constitutes his body, his congregation (I Cor. 12 : 13). The eagle first precipitates himself upon Coclès, blinding one of his eyes with his wing and at the same time painfully distinguishing him: "Beati sunt monoculi in regione caecorum," "Blessed are the one-eyed in the kingdom of the blind." Coclès objects to this kind of treatment, which he seems to conceive of both as scandalous and foolish (cf. I Cor. 1 : 23): "Mais faites donc attention! disait Coclès" (314). His inability to realize the significance of the event is equaled only by his moderation, which points to his essentially peaceful nature ("Blessed are the peacemakers," Matt. 5 : 9). Meanwhile Prometheus has opened his waistcoat and offered the bird "un morceau de son foie": "He who eats my flesh and drinks my blood has everlasting life . . ." (John 6 : 56). In passing, only Coclès has been touched by the Spirit and, it would seem, most unpleasantly at that. When the bird, metamorphosing himself into a figure of the congregation celebrating Holy Communion, then crashes on Prometheus's right side to feed on his liver—an image of solipsistic self-laceration!—the assembled guests in the café are suddenly "filled with the Holy Ghost" and begin "to speak with other tongues" (Acts 2 : 4); yet they do so without communicating. The willful and rather lukewarm reception of the Spirit results not in an illumination but in a Babylonian confusion: "Les voix sans plus d'entente aucune se diversifièrent—car d'autres étaient survenus" (314). Narcissistically, everyone listens to his own voice. The nature of the eagle is misjudged. His "shabby plumage" and his "tender but imperious chirping" are ridiculed by the audience; he is seen as "tout au plus une conscience" (314)—not a promise of paradise but, like the conscience and consciousness contracted by original sin, a threat to the potential recovery of the paradisiac state of innocence. The misunderstood gift of the Spirit is something that in Paris one immediately either sells or suffocates (315). Faced with these objections from the mocking crowd of *passants* who bypass the gift of the Spirit, even Prometheus begins to doubt the value of his eagle. The entire scene appears to be a travesty and inversion of the events reported in Acts 2 : 11, a *mise en scène* of the Gidean views on the apostles' doctrines as distortions of Christ's teachings in the dim light of their own willful, presumptuous, and limited spirit. Only Damoclès believes that he might benefit from the *tumulte grossi* by paying with his unwelcome five hundred franc note for the Communion of all involved, "trois déjeuners complets (avec conversation)" (315), as well as for the window broken by the eagle's stormy descent and for a glass eye for Coclès, leaving the remainder as a tip (*pourboire, pour boire,* most likely a bizarre figure for the priest's [the *garçon's*] drinking of the last drops of wine left over in the Communion chalice). "Puis il [Damoclès] s'enfuit béatifié" (315). The restaurant is vacated, the fleeing Damoclès, who hopes to be rid of Zeus's gift, believes that he is now "beatified," a martyr who has paid for everyone's debts ("Damoclès avait tout payé," 315), identifying himself with the redeemer (*agnus Dei qui tollit peccata mundi*; "the lamb of God that taketh away the sins of the world"). Prometheus takes leave of Coclès and the *garçon*. He slowly returns to the heights of the Caucasus, there to ponder whether he ought to sell, suffocate, or perhaps even tame his eagle—the latter representing at the same time the misunderstood spirit of his message and the selfishly ignorant congregation, his Church that is devouring his vital substance.

"La Détention de Prométhée" may be seen first as indigestion caused by the Eucharist, the aftereffects of the spiritual food inside the disunited body of the communicants, although the Lord, "lifted up" to the heights of the Caucasus (in the spirit of Calvinism), has escaped the fate of the Eucharist, oral consumption (*manducatio oralis*), and transubstantiation. It does explain the simultaneity of Prometheus's sudden return to the Caucasus and of his imprisonment after the *garçon* had denounced him. Secondly, the detention may be seen as the theological attempt to incarcerate in history, in the *saeculum*, the Incarnate Word, the extrahistorical Logos. Prometheus's discourse, made during his detention in the *salle des nouvelles lunes* to a splintered and skeptical audience that is unreceptive to the Spirit, remains as unsuccessful an undertaking as was the tempestuous descent of the eagle among the distracted communicants in the restaurant. After the exposition of Prometheus's two main points, "premier point: il faut avoir un aigle. Deuxième point: D'ailleurs, nous en avons tous un" (321), his speech quite logically leads to a *petitio principii* ("La Pétition de principes," 321f.). For Prometheus's argument that the eagle satisfies his temperament begs the questions of the bird's necessity and of his redeeming virtue for those whom he devours. Since Prometheus is unable to prove the necessity for

his eagle, or to explain the bird's origins and nature, the audience is bored and annoyed by his fiery plea that everyone
ought to love his own eagle, so that it might grow strong and
beautiful instead of degenerating into a mere conscience.
Even the pyrotechnical distractions which the speaker offers
for the amusement of his public, the *fusées volantes* (these
"cloven tongues like as of fire"), cannot dispel the general
reaction of boredom and mockery. Only Damoclès is painfully affected by this second outpouring of the Holy Ghost
(as was Coclès by the first one): "Mais Damoclès prit froid
en sortant de la salle" (327). His cold brings with it a sudden
cooling down of his blessed fervor; doubts overcome him
with regard to his "beatification." He is overpowered henceforth by his ever-increasing anguish about the five hundred
francs, which he feels he must keep so as to return them to
their rightful owner, while fears of complications arising
from his incomprehensible attachment to Coclès further undermine his rapidly declining health.

Coclès and Damoclès, the divided congregation, are incapable of efficiently communing and communicating with
Prometheus. Prometheus often visits the suffering Damoclès
but "Il ne lui parlait pas chaque fois" (330); his sporadic
presence is felt, and so is his frequent unwillingness to manifest himself, the cryptic silence of *praescientia*, foreknowledge. At least the *garçon* provides Damoclès, who is devoured
by anxieties ("l'inquiétude le dévore," 330), with the "good
news," the *evangelion*, the Gospels: "Mais du moins le garçon lui [à Damoclès] donnait des nouvelles" (330).

The Eucharist taken without grace gives Damoclès indigestion. For three days now the delirious Damoclès has
been fasting in the belief that he has eaten the five hundred
franc note, his unrecognized ticket to salvation, by paying
for everyone at the communal meal in the restaurant. He

looks for the note everywhere, without catching sight of it. He even purges himself, thinking that he might find it in his stool: "Le sort de son billet le tourmente; il le cherche partout et ne le revoit nulle part; il croit l'avoir mangé, se purge et pense le trouver dans ses selles" (330). The gift of grace, received without grace in a misunderstood Eucharist ("Damoclès avait tout payé," 315), lies heavily on his stomach. He can neither return it, nor pay for it, nor pass it on to Coclès. The gift of grace and the Eucharist are two aspects of one and the same anxiety: threatened by the sword hanging by a hair over his head Damoclès cannot peacefully enjoy the beatifying food at his Lord's banquet, nor can he digest it ("I came not to send peace, but a sword," Matt. 10 : 34). Damoclès is mentally afraid of the irrational paradox inherent in a gift that is not truly a gift, given, moreover, by an unknown giver, and his delusions as to how he should deal with it. He fails to see that the "redemption" of the unmerited banknote could not redeem his debt but only its humble acceptance: "Sauvé!! Gratuitement, fortuitement, providentiellement" (331), he raves in retrospect when thinking of his unsuccessful attempt in the restaurant to rid himself of the five hundred francs as gratuitously (*gratis, gratiis*) as he had received them (against his will), "vais-je glisser ma somme dans l'interstice de ces événements. Plus de dette! Sauvé!" (331) Filled with this hope, he mistakes the possibility of redeeming the bank note for a potential work of grace and providence. Close to death, however, he concludes: "Ah! Messieurs! quelle erreur. . . . C'est de ce jour que j'agonise" (331). He now seems to understand, in a Calvinist sense, the consequences of the misused Eucharist: the bank note was the pledge, the security given by the Spirit; the symbolic reenactment of the Last Supper was the token and seal which, if properly used, would have given what they announced, but not to Damoclès, the heretical participant.

3. Coclès and Damoclès: Literal-Minded Fools for the Sake of Christ

The anguished Damoclès lies on his deathbed, while Coclès reaches the climax of success and of self-satisfaction (332): "Voilà bien le sort de qui s'est enrichi par la souffrance d'un autre," exclaims Coclès, self-righteously condemning Damoclès. He judges without fearing that he too will be judged (Matt. 7 : 1). From time to time he still suffers a little from Damoclès's gift, his glass eye, a deceptively brilliant but blind substitute for the eye of which he was deprived by the eagle's wing. But he no longer feels the *brûlure* of the *gifle*, a sign both of his fall and of his "road to Damascus" experience. Of the slap, he reassures Prometheus, "Je ne voudrais pas ne pas l'avoir reçue . . . elle m'a révélé ma bonté. . . . Je ne cesse pas de songer que ma douleur servit à mon prochain de provende et qu'elle lui valut cinq cents francs" (333). Coclès, in his presumption, sees in the blow which Zeus had dealt him a mysterious sign of his election. To Damoclès's literal-minded concepts of his guilt and of his gift of the glass eye to Coclès corresponds Coclès's literal-minded zeal that leaves him indifferent to the consequences of his cherished martyrdom, to which Damoclès owes both his five hundred francs and their fatal effects on his peace of mind, his health, and his very survival. Coclès is so deeply moved by his own natural bounty, his charity, and his willingness to sacrifice himself again for some other Damoclès that he entirely overlooks how fatally his unwanted good deed (for which he is scarcely responsible) has affected the first Damoclès. It is almost as though he saw Damoclès's fate only through the blind glass eye which the latter himself had bought for him. He attributes Damocles's death to Prometheus's doctrine of the necessity under which each man exists to feed his own eagle. Now, however, Prometheus himself washes his hands of his former teachings, explaining that Damoclès acted counter to the Promethean spirit, occupying a viewpoint diametrically opposed to it: "Que voulez-vous? Damoclès et moi, nous n'avons jamais pu nous entendre; nos points de vue sont diamétralement opposés" (333), he declares to Coclès. Damoclès had obstinately followed the letter, not the spirit, in everything, ever since he had submitted the envelope containing the five hundred francs to the graphologists' analysis; to his bitter end he had clung to literal interpretations of the Word, in the strictest Calvinist tradition. He misinterpreted the Scriptures by believing he had augmented his debt by passing it on to Coclès: "Coclès! il ne t'appartient pas, ton œil, puisque ne m'appartient pas la somme avec quoi je te l'ai donné. 'Qu'as-tu donc que tu n'aies reçu,' dit l'Ecriture . . . ," he quotes Paul (I Cor. 4 : 7). But he leads his pathetic quotation *ad absurdum* by the desperate outcry of his disbelief, by his stubborn quest for his creditor whose existence is as much of a stumbling block to him as is his impenetrable anonymity: "reçu de qui [cinq cents francs]? de qui?? de Qui??" (332) The triple question, thrice repeated during the scene, and the last capitalized 'Qui??" would seem to hint at the mystery of the Trinity which—even taken as a mystery— must remain forever unacceptable, unrevealed to Damoclès's rationalist literal-mindedness. Likewise Prometheus had temporarily lost faith in himself (when his eagle was silent), but he had regained his composure, his belief in himself as the Incarnate Logos, and continued his discourse (325). Contrary to Prometheus's doubts, which in a Cartesian manner led to self-knowledge (and were possibly uttered to mystify the audience), Damoclès's ravings explain why—in a Calvinist sense—he is lacking true knowledge of God: he neither knows himself nor the meaning of his call—self-knowledge and knowledge of God being interdependent (*Institutio* I, 1). What bothers Damoclès most is the "unconverted" Coclès

who ought to suffer burning pains from his glass eye—a hint
at Coclès's unmerited vision of God, a revelation to which
natural man should be blind. "Mais ton œil te brûle, Coclès," he admonishes him with proselytizing zeal, "j'en suis
sûr il te brûle, ton œil de verre; arrache-le!" (332) His allusion to Matthew 18 : 9 suggests an analogy between this
practically nonexistent *brûlure* and the flames of hell: "And
if thine eye offend thee, pluck it out, and cast it from thee:
it is better for thee to enter into life with one eye, rather
than having two eyes to be cast into hell fire." But Coclès
is already one-eyed, due to the eagle's intervention; and his
glass eye he owes to Damoclès, who had paid for it with a
portion of Zeus's gift which, in turn, had come to him through
Coclès's haphazard mediation. Frustrated by Coclès's insensitivity to the *brûlure* that he ought to feel (an insensitivity
which he mistakes for a stubborn refusal to receive his [Damo-
clès's] catechization), Damoclès obstinately insists with missionary bathos: "S'il ne te brûle pas [l'œil de verre], il devrait
te brûler" (332). He misinterprets the nature of this *brûlure*,
for Coclès a purely temporary fervor (now almost fully dis-
sipated and never quite understood by Coclès) caused by
the eagle when, in his role as the Holy Ghost, he had so bru-
tally lit upon him. "Et s'il [l'œil de verre] n'est pas à toi, il
est donc à ton frère. Il est à qui? à qui?? à Qui??" (332) The
triple exorcism of Coclès—futile, desperate, founded upon
the foolish attempt to penetrate with rational means a mystery pertaining to faith—is followed by the almost blasphemous exorcism of *Deus ignotus*, Zeus, the banker, the "Miglionnaire," giver of unrequested gifts that prove gratuitous,
as useless as the five hundred franc note and what it was
able to buy: an ineffective Eucharist; a glass eye for Coclès;
anguish and sickness unto death for Damoclès.

The theatrical death of Damoclès, played before Coclès,
the *garçon*, and Prometheus, illustrates the Pauline teaching:

"For I think that God hath set forth us the apostles last, as it were appointed to death (*tanquam morti destinatos*): for we are made a spectacle unto the world, and to angels, and to men" (I Cor. 4 : 9). A spectacle, a *sotie*: "We are fools for Christ's sake (*nos stulti propter Christum*)" (I Cor. 4 : 10). Damoclès's apostleship fails; not recognizing his gift, nor its origin, he dies in selfish indignation about Coclès's stubborn refusal to be converted by him, to give up whatever little he has been given (a glass eye) in return for his vital loss. Damoclès, in the name of the unknown giver, dies "angry with his brother" (Matt. 5 : 22), transforming Coclès into the image of the "blessed," according to the Sermon on the Mount: for "poor in spirit," "mourning," "meek," "hungering and thirsting for righteousness," a "peacemaker," Coclès is "persecuted for righteousness' sake" and "reviled," because Damoclès indeed "says all manner of evil against him" for the Lord's sake (cf. Matt. 5 : 3-12). Damoclès dies, torn by doubts as to whether his prayers will be heard: "Again I say unto you; That if two of you shall agree on earth as touching any thing that they shall ask, it shall be done for them of my Father which is in heaven" (Matt. 18 : 19). Yet, explains the narrator, "la fin de Damoclès fut admirable; il eut, peu avant sa dernière heure, de ces paroles qui arrachent des larmes aux impies, font dire aux bien-pensants qu'elles étaient édifiantes" (333). Damoclès's misunderstood self-mortification, a spectacle edifying the *bien-pensants*, is quite literally a suicide (*mortificatio* being compounded of *mors* plus *ficere*, *mortem facere*, a killing, a putting to death). Out of Damoclès's mortification comes Coclès's vivification. Damoclès, mortified, dies in doubts, under the sword of his anguish. His edifying last words express fear that he might have deprived "Celui . . . celui qui m'a donné . . . quelque chose" (333). "Non! C'etait le Bon Dieu, riposta habilement le garçon" (333), perhaps more rhetorically than out of conviction, as indicated by the excessive vivacity (implied by *riposta*) and cleverness of his reply (suggested by *habilement*), aimed primarily at consoling the dying Damoclès. His answer, however, does not seem to offer much of a consolation to the moribund patient, for it leaves open the question whether Damoclès had successfully paid for everything and everyman *ad medicationem futurae vitae*, "for the cure which is the life to come" (Calvin, *Institutio* III, 9), or whether he was unable to deliver himself of the five hundred francs precisely because they were meant to bring him *perditio*, "bankruptcy," perdition, hopelessness, a sense of total loss: "He that findeth his life shall lose it: and he that loseth his life for my sake shall find it" (Matt. 10 : 39). Be this as it may, "Damoclès mourut sur cette bonne parole" (333), without knowing whether he will be saved, but listening to the name of God ("c'était le Bon Dieu") and to the Gospel, the *evangelion*, "cette bonne parole," brought to him by the *garçon*. But the "bonne parole" seems to bode nothing good for him. The *garçon's* reassuring words that the five hundred francs belonged to God Almighty only sound like a disquieting echo of Paul's rhetorical question, directed by Damoclès to Coclès: "Qu'as-tu donc que tu n'aies reçu?" (332; I Cor. 4 : 7), a reproach which is preceded in the same verse by a question which faces the key problems of grace, predestination, and perdition, the primary mystery of faith as the precondition for grace: "For who maketh thee to differ from another?" To this question the fool Damoclès knows no answer. He may well hear before his death the name of God and the "good word," testimony of the Holy Ghost (*testimonium Spiritus sancti*, Calvin, *Institutio* I, 7), but for him this is not a good omen. He is caught in the vicious circle of the Calvinist concepts of grace and predestination. His seemingly hopeless condition, as well as his evil, his mortal sickness which brings him to fall, were predestined from the beginning of time, like the fall and road of Damascus experience of Coclès, struck down by Zeus and then again visited by the wing of the eagle that Zeus had sent out to devour and tempt Prometheus: "Hence Man falls, according to what God had ordained: but he falls through his own vice" (Calvin, *Institutio* III, 23, 8).

4. *Prometheus Unbound*

Profoundly touched by the death of Damoclès (to whom his discourse had given the final blow, Prometheus now admits: "J'étais si convaincu" (334); an ambiguous confession since *convaincu* means both "convinced" and "convicted." His persuasion that one must feed his own eagle had literally detained him in the body of a frigid and indifferent community. In this sense the misunderstood visitation by the Holy Ghost had turned for everyone concerned into the experience of the devouring eagle—as consciousness of guilt and convicting bad conscience; as the fateful sword suspended over Damoclès's head ever since he was called (Matt. 10 : 34); as the eagle's memorable wing-stroke which had cost Coclès one eye. Prometheus's discourse too, in the end, had been no more than an *acte gratuit*, in a literal sense, a gratuitous act, and figuratively, the disinterested but creative Word that was to seal the death of Damoclès after which Prometheus avows: "J'ai d'autres idées sur mon aigle" (334). In a way, this revelation is a tacit condemnation of all narrow-minded and unilateral types of exegesis. It applies not only to Damoclès but also to Coclès's self-righteous claims to natural goodness, just as it fits his untiring zeal in offering his other cheek to procure *provende* for his neighbor, whosoever he may be, regardless of whether such *praebenda* may cause an indigestion with fatal effects. Above all, however, Prometheus's change of mind represents a powerful argument for freedom, casting doubt upon the very premises of the Calvinist doctrine of predestination. For now it is clear that, from the very beginning, Prometheus had a free choice of either fattening his eagle at the expense of his own vitality or of becoming himself *gras, frais,* and—to the annoyance of his audience—*souriant,* by shaking off his eagle, or at least by not feeding him.

It is in this spirit of liberation that Prometheus begins his funeral oration for Damoclès not by praising the defunct but with an obscure prophecy of freedom and eternal life, in the words of Matthew 8 : 22: "Laissez les morts ensevelir les morts. Nous ne nous occuperons donc plus de Damoclès" (335). Damoclès's death had resulted from his lack of faith in the freedom that had been offered him; all the worse for him! He had failed to see the νῦν, the beginning of the new aeon right here and now (John 4 : 14, 6 : 51, 11 : 26; II Cor. 5 : 17, etc.); he was unaware of his calling to be among those who have (John 3 : 15; 5 : 24, etc.); he had given up life right now, *et nunc,* in his perpetual fear of the "sword of the Spirit," Paul's concept of the "word of God" (Eph. 6 : 17). In his exclusive care for his own very particular eagle, in his dutiful fear of perdition, he had lost all appetite for the banquet of life at the very thought of his supposed indebtedness, so that death must have appeared to him as a welcome redeemer from his incessant cares and worries.

"La dernière fois que je vous vis réunis c'était pour m'entendre parler de mon aigle," continues Prometheus; "Damoclès en est mort; laissons les morts . . ." (335). Buried with Damoclès is the Pauline and Calvinist spirit of a devouring fear of life, conscience and consciousness of guilt. Released with this burial is the free, creative, and self-creative *acte gratuit* of a divine fire and *ferveur* which are offered mankind now that Prometheus himself has recovered his freedom. This he gained by killing his eagle, which had been the incarnation of his bad conscience and of life-destroying knowledge, of theological self-satisfaction, of the rationalized death wishes inherent in the selfish congregation, and in its Calvinist *Institution*. Through Damoclès's death Prometheus gains the grace of realizing his freedom: "C'est à cause de lui [Damoclès] pourtant, ou plutôt c'est grâce à sa mort qu'à présent j'ai tué mon aigle . . ." (335). Damoclès had personified the fear of life. His anguished selfishness represented ideas petrified in ecclesiastical institutions which, like the congregation itself, willfully but unfreely ate the *panis vitae*, the bread of life, without uniting with it, without communing, without giving up their self-seeking ends and their fears of the beyond—in brief, without joyfully entering into the common body of life.

Three. "HISTOIRE DE TITYRE"

1. In Many a Glass Darkly: Gide's Mirror Technique

THE LITERARY *sotie* is formally added to the theological one in "Histoire de Tityre," the anecdotal digression to Prometheus's funeral oration on Damoclès. It reveals a multiple narcissism, a technique of ironic self-reflections *ad infinitum* of the *Prométhée*'s major themes and protagonists in the hall of mirrors of literary allusions, which evoke in the reader's mind associations as numerous as the enticements of Echo the nymph. From Gide's previous works now emerge parabolical figures who owe their names, as well as clues to their character, to Virgil's *Bucolica*. Tityre (*Paludes*) and Ménalque (*Les Nourritures terrestres*) are joined by Moelibée. With their aid and with that of Angèle (also borrowed from *Paludes*), Prometheus as a fictitious narrator within the framework of the main narrative holds up a parabolical mirror to the moral of the *sotie*, which adds one more reflection to the labyrinthine mirror system of the *Prométhée*. Tityre's original care for his oak corresponds to Prometheus's love for his eagle who, like the oak, is consecrated in Greek and Roman mythology to Zeus-Iuppiter as the divine bird par excellence (Aristotle *Historia animalium* 9. 32 *fin.*).

The parable of Tityre and his oak tree figuratively demonstrates the disquieting consequences of an *acte gratuit* whose divine origin is questionable. Its author, we are told, is Ménalque, who had played in *Les Nourritures terrestres* (and will play again in *L'Immoraliste*) the ambiguous role of the amoral redeemer-seducer. In Virgil's *Eclogues* his skin is dark (*niger, Ecl.* 2. 16) like that of the fallen Lucifer, and

87

Manoetas apostrophizes him as "perverse Menalca" (*Ecl.*
3. 13). It is Ménalque who plants two seeds, one growing
into an oak in Tityre's swamp, the other into an idea in
Tityre's mind (335).[1] Ménalque's planted grains recall Zeus's
illusory gifts to man and his cynical remark to the *garçon*,
"Ce que je plante en l'homme, je m'amuse à ce que cela
pousse" (329). They are the equivalent of the eagle eggs
hidden by Zeus in everyone's breast. The seeds correspond to
each other. Tityre sacrifices to both of them his freedom
and his innocence, and both are meant to trap and enslave
him. With Tityre's questionable possession by which he is
obsessed, with his tree of sorrows and its dubious origins,
doubts are also cast upon the value, validity, and divine
origins of the Promethean eagle and indirectly upon the
history of Church and civilization, upon dogmata, Calvinist
repressions, and puritanical asceticism. These doubts are
suggested in the spirit of Gide's answer given a decade later
to Joseph de Maistre's well-known maxim: "Ce qui gêne
l'homme le fortifie." Yes, agrees Gide, provided one can shake
off these restraints which, more often than not, threaten to
suffocate those who are inhibited by them: "C'est en s'échappant au calvinisme et seulement en s'en échappant et souvent
en se retournant contre lui, que ces romanciers ont pu ré-
ussir" (*J.* 1, 351f.) he concludes, in referring to the heroism
with which Thackeray and other English Puritan writers had
fought their inbred inhibitions.

"Histoire de Tityre" indeed illustrates the moral of the
Prométhée. Tityre's oak is like Prometheus's eagle, a complex
image for the Church and for Calvinist pessimism, for the
Calvinist conscience which is "bad" even when it seems to
be "good" and, as self-righteousness, stresses one's neighbor's
guilt while fearfully rejoicing over the narrow escape one had

[1] On a more literal level of interpretation, "Histoire de Tityre" para-
phrases I Cor. 3 : 5-4 : 13; Ménalque represents St. Paul, Tityre Apollos.

from succumbing to the temptations which have entrapped the sinful. Both Tityre's tree and Prometheus's devouring bird of prey stand for the historical consciousness of evil inherent in all spontaneous acts which are not rooted in the depth of a sense of duty, not conceived of as *dettes* and *devoirs*. In short, "Histoire de Tityre" allegorizes on the moral level the paralyzing fear of liberating *actions gratuites* and, on the aesthetic plane, the hesitations before the divine freedom of creative *actes gratuits*. Now man too is capable of gratuitous acts provided that, freed from the shackles of orthodoxy and morality, he assumes the role of the artist, communicating in his work his intimate vision of a universe all his own—a gratuitous vision, for it seems to obey no external necessity except for that imposed by the laws of an artistic form which organically creates its own object. But at the same time "Histoire de Tityre" holds up a distorting mirror to the historicity of Coclès and Damoclès. Each one's *histoire* affects with the force of determinism his conscience and consciousness, driving both of these comedians, who are too serious for their roles, dutifully to pursue the respective lots which were so fortuitously played into their hands. For Damoclès, this parabolical mirror reflects his destiny when it is too late for him to benefit from the lesson which, in an almost Brechtian way, it shows without interpreting. Coclès, without understanding this lesson, by the grace of Prometheus is made to avail himself of its blessings, which in the end guarantee him freedom, redemption, salvation—his release from the yoke of history.

Prometheus's attitude toward his eagle, the relationship between Damoclès and his unwanted five hundred franc note, the rapports between Coclès and the divine slap as well as his glass eye for which Damoclès had paid with someone else's money, and finally the chiasmic interplay of the protagonists in the main narrative are once more reflected in the story of

Tityre and his tree, an anecdote which exemplifies an idea (Ménalque's seed planted in Tityre's mind) congealed into an institution (Calvin's *Christianae religionis Institutio*; the oak tree planted by Ménalque in Tityre's swamp). Its systematization enslaves its owner in the service of a sense of duty, of indebtedness toward a possession which undermines his health and his freedom in the name of a growing tradition, of historical consciousness, and of the bad conscience inherited from original sin, from the knowledge of good and evil.

"Histoire de Tityre" projects its ironical mirror-image beyond the framework of the *Prométhée* into Gide's bitter controversy with the political right wing of France over Maurice Barrès's questionable thesis on *déracinement* in the course of which Gide proved to be by far the better botanist. Tityre's stagnation in his morass, his morbid rootedness in his property—first, in his identification with his oak, whose care devours his vitality, and then again, in his native swamp— underscores Gide's devastating answer to the thesis advanced in Barrès's *Les Déracinés* (1897). There the problems of decadence had been related to uprootedness, to the desertion of the native soil by young provincials who felt attracted by the glamour of Paris, and to the supposedly noxious influence by transplanted aliens (and Jews) upon the life of the nation (cf. *M.ch.*, 14ff.).

2. Nomina, Noumina, *or What's in a Name?*

The names of the protagonists to some extent explain the close associations which exist between the moral and the literary allusions. Mirror-images of a polymorphously reflected model are superimposed in the character of Tityre. As already shown, the *Prométhée*'s Tityre points through his namesake in *Paludes* (1895) to Virgil's bucolic Tityrus. *Paludes*, explains the writer-hero of *Paludes*, reporting in the first person singular, "c'est l'histoire d'un homme qui, possédant le champ de Tityre, ne s'efforce pas d'en sortir, mais au contraire s'en contente" (91). To make sure that his reader will associate Tityre with Virgil's Tityrus, the narrator places before this comment Meliboeus's apostrophe to Tityrus:

> Et tibi magna satis quamvis lapis omnia nudus
> Limosoque palus obducat pascua junco. . . .
>
> *(Ecl.* 1, 48f.)

(You put up with naked rocks / and muddy marshland pastures invaded by rush. . . .)

Here, as in Gide's *Paludes* and "Histoire de Tityre," the protagonist lives surrounded by swamps. In *Paludes*, Gide's fictitious narrator in turn uses Tityre as the fictitious narrator of a *tiroir* story *Paludes*; like its author and Virgil's Tityrus, Tityre cannot get on in his endeavors, since he is literally stuck in the morass of his properties, of his idiosyncrasy which he has chosen as the very topic of his work and whence he cannot move on. Servius sees in Tityrus a mask for the poet himself: "hoc loco Tityri sub persona Vergilium debemus accipere" ("In this passage, we must perceive Virgil under the mask of Tityrus," *Comm. en Verg. Buc.* 1. 1). Tityre means *satyros* (Aelianus *Varia Hist.* 3. 40), "billy goat," "bellwether," and is derived from τίτος ("little bird," a euphemistic metaphor for "phallus") and τύλος (*membrum virile*), with the root tŭ (to swell) (cf. Roscher). But Gide's Tityre is the very opposite of potency and virility, for he plays the piteous role of a writer impotent in his attempts to come to grips with his topic. The theme of *Paludes* is that of his professional incompetence, a stagnation in good intentions which results in the noncomposition of his projected work of pure art, *Paludes*. Last but not least, *Paludes* parodies with

Gidean perfidy Mallarmé's obsession with the paralyzing
purity of the *page blanche*, the innocent white sheet of paper
which, as yet unviolated, latently contains the infinite possibilities of *le Poème*. This derision seems to be discreetly
echoed by the pilgrimage of Moelibée, who—with the nudity
of the innocent pagan—plays his primitive shepherd's flute
until, face to face with Tityre, his instrument, the τιτύρος [!]
is reduced to the Mallarméan music of silence. On the level
of literary satire, Moelibée's *eo Romam* can hardly be misunderstood as an allusion to Mallarmé's *mardis*, held in his
salon, 89 rue de Rome, so ardently frequented by Gide, Pierre
Louÿs, and Valéry. The rue de Rome is relatively close to the
scene of the *Prométhée*, the "boulevard qui mène de la
Madeleine" (read "from the sin committed against the vir-
ginal page of white paper") "à l'Opéra" ("to the temple for
Wagner's *Musikdrama*," the total work of art competing with
the total poem of Mallarmé, the amateur of *la musique du
silence*).

> Tityre, tu patulae recubans sub tegmine fagi
> siluestrem tenui musam meditaris auena;
> nos patriae finis et dulcia linquimus arua;
> nos patriam fugimus; tu, Tityre, lentus in umbra,
> formosam resonare doces Amaryllida siluas.
> (Virgil *Ecl.* 1. 1ff.)

> (Tityrus, you recline beneath the shade of the wide-
> spreading beech / Thinking with your shepherd's pipe
> to charm the woodland muse, / While we must leave
> behind our homeland's sweet meadows. / We flee our
> homeland; but you, o Tityrus, lazing in the shade /
> Teach the woods to echo "fair Amaryllis.")

Virgil's *Bucolica* begin with the vocative *Tityre*, the com-
plaint of the uprooted Meliboeus, and the image of Tityrus,

the freedman who has found peace in his swampy wasteland where he is resting in the shade of his *fagus*, Hellenized perhaps as an oak (the Doric is φαγός [cf. Theocritus 9. 20] and δρῦς αγρία, the Latin *quercus aegilops*, belonging to the oak family). It is of some interest to the relationship between Tityre's oak and Prometheus's eagle in Gide's *Prométhée* that the Doric φαγός (Attic φηγός) had already been derived from φαγεῖν, "to eat," by Hellenic and Hellenistic etymologists.[2]

"Au commencement était Tityre" (335). The very first sentence of "Histoire de Tityre" literally points to the very first word of Virgil's first *Eclogue*. More ironically and with greater transparency it seems to allude to the first sentence in the Gospel according to St. John: "In principio erat Verbum ("In the beginning was the Word," John 1 : 1). The Tityre of *Paludes* who, to begin with, parodies Virgil's Tityrus, acquires an added dimension in Prometheus's funeral oration for Damoclès on the theme, "Let the dead bury their dead" (Matt. 8 : 22). In *Paludes*, Tityre had served as a sort of fictitious stand-in, a deputy, for the fictitious narrator; he was deputized to write *Paludes*, the stagnating *livre à tiroirs*, a task too hard to be completed by either the fictitious nar-

---

[2] On *fagus*, φαγεῖν, see also Servius, *Comm. in Verg. Buc.* 1. 1:

Quod autem eum [Tityrum] sub fago dicit iacere, allegoria est honestissima, quasi sub arbore glandifera, quae fuit victus causa: antea enim homines glandibus vescebantur, unde etiam fagus dicta est ἀπό τοῦ φαγεῖν. hoc videtur dicere: iaces sub umbra fagi in agris tui, tuas retentans possessiones, quibus aleris, sicut etiam glandibus alebantur ante mortales.

(Thus, he says, he [Tityrus] is lying under a *fagus*: a most appropriate allegory, for it is as though he were lying under an acorn-bearing tree, the producer of basic foodstuff. In bygone days, men ate acorns, whence it is still said about the *fagus*, ἀπό τοῦ φαγεῖν. The verse clearly means: You are lying in the shade of your *fagus* in your field, keeping the goods by which you eat, just as primitive men fed on acorns.)

rator or his fictitious stand-in. Prometheus's Tityre turns into
an allegory of the historical stand-in for Christ on earth, of
the earthly deputy of the Incarnate Word whose message of
eternal life, *et nunc*, is gradually lost with the growth of the
"tree," the ecclesiastical theology of the cross, its civilizing
historicity and life-suffocating institutions. Servius, in a vari-
ant of his commentary on Virgil (edited by P. Daniel in
1600), innocently suggests these associations (so fruitful for
the Christian reader), calling Tityre's *fagus "arbor crux"*
(cross, thus torment, torture, etc., *Comm. in Verg. Ecl.* 1. 1).
Tityre, who "was in the beginning," may be related to his
oak in a manner analogous to Plutarch's Arcadians who, according to legend, were supposed to have sprung from the
earth like the first tree, the oak (Plutarch *Quaest. rom.* 92).
To recapitulate, like the Platonic Idea and its earthly copy,
Tityre's care for the tree and the tree itself spring from two
grains which Ménalque, the tempter, had simultaneously
planted in Tityre's swamp and in his mind. Both grow, we are
told, "avec l'aide de Dieu" (335) like the grain of mustard
seed in the parable on the kingdom of heaven (Matt. 13 :
31). They do so, to be sure, at Tityre's expense, as Prometheus had likewise wasted away while fattening his eagle, and
Damoclès had found death while mortifying himself over
Zeus's unmerited gift to him. Tityre cares exclusively for his
tree, organizing and maintaining the complex institutions
needed to protect its growth. In his total commitment to the
divine oak he can be likened to Damoclès seeking to penetrate
the mystery surrounding the true owner of the five hundred
franc note, to Coclès zealously engaged in the quest for another divine slap in his face, and, of course, to Prometheus
feeding his eagle. For Tityre's oak fully corresponds in its
mythological attributes and connotations to Prometheus's
eagle: we have seen that both are consecrated to Zeus (Virgil
Georg. 3. 332; *Aen.* 3. 680); the oak is Zeus's oracular tree

(Cicero *Att.* 2. 4, 5; Virgil *Georg.* 2. 16; 3. 332; Ovid *Met.* 7. 623; 8. 716), the eagle is his oracular bird (Homer *Il.* 8. 247; 24. 315; Aristotle *Hist. anim.* 8. 18 *fin.*).

The oak, with whose interests Tityre identifies his own cares, becomes his tormenting spirit, as the eagle—in primitive mythologies the original fire-thief who brings the divine fire of the sun to man—was first identified with Prometheus, and then became his god-appointed tormentor: "When for the eagle, *prometheus* (far-seeing, a name given to the eagle as a bird of augury), men substituted the Titan, Prometheus, the eagle remained in the legend, but as executioner instead of victim."[3] Tityre's oak is his burden, his cross. Its strong roots dry out the surrounding soil, so that "Tityre eut un sol ferme où poser ses pieds, reposer sa tête et fortifier l'ouvrage de ses mains" (335). An entry in Gide's diaries, written approximately at the time of the *Prométhée*, tells us what he purported to think about earthly ties and possessions, rootedness in tradition and in the native soil, comfort and cares for possessions. The words of Christ, he says, freed from their apostolic misinterpretations, "paraîtront plus dramatiquement, niant enfin la famille . . . , tirant l'homme lui-même de son milieu pour une carrière personnelle"—the *idiosyncrasie* sought by the passersby on the "boulevard qui mène de la Madeleine à l'Opéra!—"et lui enseignant par son exemple et sa voix [ceux du Christ] à n'avoir plus de possessions sur la terre, plus de lieu où reposer sa tête. O avènement de cet état nomade, toute mon âme te souhaite" (*J.* 1, 96; "Morale chrétienne" 1896–). Gide himself has often cautioned us not to pay too much attention to his religious outpourings (see in particular his correspondence with Claudel, and especially the passages on *Numquid et tu . . . ?*). The theatrical tone of "Morale chrétienne" is in itself suspect, and suggests rhetori-

[3] Salomon Reinach, *Orpheus: A History of Religions*, trans. Florence Simmonds (New York, 1930), p. 90.

cal exercises in fictitious emotions and religious self-dramatization rather than thought born from the spontaneity and
authenticity of religious fervor. These suspicions are strength-
ened by the not very prepossessing avarice of André Gide the
man. But we are not concerned with Gide's personal sincerity; it is the writer who interests us both as a novelist and
a theorist. His dramatizations of religious thought, as they
occur in his essays and diaries, are literary phenomena throw-
ing light on the true meaning not of his life but of his fiction.
Gide's diaries, in a way, are the palimpsest underlying his
plays, his novels, *récits*, *soties*, and essays; they are a barely
hidden commentary on his artistic efforts and achievements,
and for this reason only we refer to them. The text just
quoted is accompanied by a number of New Testament passages directed against property, personal possessions, and the
institution of the family. Among those biblical quotations
one again finds the verse chosen by Prometheus (Matt. 8 :
22) as the basis for his funeral oration on Damoclès. They all
stress the joyful message of the New Testament, which elimi-
nates mourning, care for possessions and family, and establishes the universality of communal bonds of love among all
humankind, not in heaven, but on earth (*J.* 1, 94).

The message of love and of Gidean *dénuement*, of the
ideal nomadic life, is embodied by Moelibée. He is the exact
opposite of Tityre, rooted with his oak in the soil of his
swamp. Tityre owes to the idea planted in him by Ménalque
and to "God's aid" the "firm soil under his feet," the "place
to rest his head," the "fortifications" of the *Ecclesia militans*
which he protectively erects around his tree of sorrows.

Decades after the *Prométhée*, when suggesting that there is
no true work of art "sans participation démoniaque" (*Dostoïevsky*, 200), Gide draws the aesthetic lesson from the polarity of themes which pervades his entire work: an ironic pen-
dulum movement between *ferveur et dénuement sacrés* and

ferveur et dénuement profanes, two emotional states of self-deception, the comedy of religious and sensual fervor and destitute readiness, played by essentially arid characters *au coeur sec* in a desperate search for sensations of sainthood or for the warmth of carnal love—a comedy well-known to André Gide, the man, who in his life and his fiction has enacted it over and over again.[4] Without hubris and self-deception, without the collaboration of demonic and diabolical forces, Gide's protagonists, like Gide himself, cannot attain the experience of holiness in their artificially created hothouse climate of religious pseudoenthusiasm (cf. *El Hadj, La Porte étroite, La Symphonie pastorale, Le Retour de l'enfant prodigue,* etc.). In Gide's work and life there seems to be no dividing line between sincerity and unconscious hypocrisy, the farce of sainthood and a demonic obsession that is mistaken for sanctity, or even identical with it. Likewise Gide's physically sick heroes are cured only if they forsake tradition and engage in capricious and dangerous *actes gratuits.* They must enter into a complicity with evil, make a pact with the devil. To renew themselves, they must expel their acquired second nature by returning to their first one, to their innocent Arcadian id in its full amorality, in its freedom from enslavement by history and ideologies, and in its hostility toward civilization. The cure carries the risk of a plunge into atavism from which may emerge a blasphemous distortion of the new man promised by the Gospels (398f.), the total barbarian (as callous and arid as Gide's false saints), Michel, the hero of *L'Immoraliste.* Gide's abysmal irony commands that their vitalistic and saintly attempts alike

---

[4] Gide's differentiation between love and sensuality made it possible for him to entertain tender (though at times acrimonious) but unerotic relations with his wife Madeleine (Emmanuèle in his *œuvre*), throughout their long marriage, while simultaneously giving free course to his homosexual pursuits, and even having daughters of his own with Mme Théo van Rysselberghe.

must needs lead his protagonists into temptation and to unexpected goals, which more often than not are the opposite
of the state they had hoped to attain. His pale self-appointed
candidates for sanctity (*sanctitas* is the equivalent of *sanitas,*
sanctity meaning "sanity" and "health of body") must lan-
guish and die (Damoclès in the *Prométhée,* Alissa in *La
Porte étroite*), while his vitalistic immoralists, with their
immersion in the sickness of evil, find the way back to the
wholeness, the holiness of life before the fall, to the sanity
of an Eden-like indifference toward the problems of good
and evil. In *Les Nourritures terrestres,* Gide knows what he
does when he gives to the diabolical Ménalque's disciple the
name Nathanaël—Nathanael who first doubts in Christ
("And Nathanael said unto him, Can there any good
thing come out of Nazareth?" [John 1 : 46]); Nathanael who,
converted, follows the Lord as a disciple; Nathanael, whose
name means "God's gift." Gide's Nathanaël is advised to
throw away the dangerous book with the "earthly food"—
but, perfidiously, only after he has thoroughly studied it.

Ménalque's gifts to Tityre, the idea of the tree and the tree
itself, grow with God's aid into an *arbor vitae,* a tree of life
with bizarre ramifications, symbolizing the Church and its
institutions and overshadowing Tityre's existence. In Virgil's
first *Eclogue,* too, the *fagus* as a divine gift has a somewhat
relative value. Tityrus may rave, "O Melibœe, deus nobis haec
otia fecit" ("O Meliboeus, a god has given me this blessed
peace," *Ecl.* 1. 6), but his god, the divine emperor Octavian,
who gave him both freedom and property, is anything but
a divine and gracious giver for Meliboeus. Virgil's Tityrus,
transposed into Gide's *sotie,* would seem in this verse al-
legorically to render unto Caesar the things that are God's
(Matt. 22 : 21). Tityrus is addressed by Meliboeus as *fortunate senex* ("fortunate old man") (*Ecl.* 1. 46); Gide's irony
transforms Tityre's *otia,* the blessed peace of the lucky old

man, into *negotia* (*nec otia*), the grim "business" which became Adam's lot, the lot of the *vieil homme*, after his expulsion from Paradise. Tityre is weighed down by the *idée fixe*, the sense of responsibility planted in his mind by Ménalque, which turns his life into a total enslavement to the "business" of his tree, the administrative history of his oak, which with its ever increasing burden of needs figuratively represents the tree of the cross to which Tityre is nailed, as Prometheus was nailed to the rocks of Caucasus, and before him, in dim prehistory, his eagle was crucified—the Holy Ghost of prophecy whose theft of the divine fire for mankind's sake had preceded the Promethean myth in legend.

3. Quia Tu Es Petrus. . . . *And on This Rock*
I Will Build My Church

"Laconum lingua tityrus dicitur aries maior, qui gregem anteire consuevit," comments Servius ("In the language of the Lacedaemonians, the bellwether who normally leads the flock is called *tityrus*, *Verg. ecl. prooem.*). In Gide's *Prométhée*, Tityre, obsessed by the idea and the reality of his tree and committed to their care, starts out by being an allegory of the herd's bellwether, the vicar on earth of the Good Shepherd. In the course of Prometheus's anecdote, he undergoes a metamorphosis, allegorizing two stages of the Western Church. In the beginning of his *histoire* he appears as a satire on the papacy; later on he is transformed—as we shall see—into a grotesque allegory of the Reformation. In sum, the fool's play of Tityre and his oak, inserted into the framework of the *sotie*, represents the transformations of Christian civilization in the Western world, seen through Gide's colored glasses as a senseless comedy of blind zeal and errors, a lugubrious farce on the theme *plus ça change, plus c'est la même chose*. It embodies Gide's denunciation of the Church as a morass of temporizations, of secular concordats with worldly powers which dried out and evaporated the message of eternal life on the terra firma of historicity, property, and willful acquisition of earthly wealth, thus severely contradicting the Christian command to abandon all secular possessions.

"Et ego dico tibi, quia tu es Petrus, et super hanc petram aedificabo ecclesiam meam" ("So I now say to you: You are Peter and on this rock I will build my Church," (Matt. 16 : 18)—Petrus, Πέτρος, in Hebrew "Kephas," the "rock" on which the Church is to be erected. The serious pun, in Prometheus's parable, is the moral of the consequences which Ménalque's dubious gifts will have for Tityre. Both the idea of the tree and the tree itself (in a way) are prefigured by Menalca's admonition to Tityrus in Virgil's third *Eclogue*: "Tityre, coge pecus" ("Tityrus, drive together the herd!") (*Ecl.* 3. 20). Tityrus *pastor gregis*, Tityre shepherd of the congregation becomes Petrus. "Histoire de Tityre" represents quite literally Tityre entering into history, the petrifaction of Tityre, his conversion into Petrus, the "rock" of the Church, his petrification in the historical edifice of the Church in the *saeculum*, in this world. In other terms, the story of Tityre is a *sotie* within the *sotie*, allegorizing the secularization of Christianity, the Apostolic succession wholly devoted to the care of the perpetually growing tree and the rapidly spreading idea, the coalescing of idea and tree (both of dubious origins but with increasing assistance from God) in the catholic ramifications of the Church.

As the custodian and chief administrator of his tree to which he feels bound (*attaché*), Tityre institutes the closed hierarchy of ecclesiastical offices and a fixed order of rituals, eliminating spontaneity as well as chance from the exercise of religious functions. The spirit of Christ's teachings is neglected in favor of the literal observance of a minutely regulated protocol which purports to exist for the propagation of a doctrine derived from this spirit. The order of rank within the ecclesiastical establishment is as strictly observed as the minutely regulated details of the sacramental ritual: "chacun devait s'en tenir strictement à sa spécialité" (335). A severely determinist theology precludes for the faithful all pagan beliefs in fate and in the tragic sense of life on this earth. In this spirit, Tityre hires a *sarcleur* ("weeder")— Gide's way of hinting at the parable of the sower and the seed (Matt. 13 : 24ff.). It is his task, presumably, to gather the enemy's tares, which symbolize the "children of the wicked," the nonbelievers, and to cast them "into the furnace of fire; there shall be wailing and gnashing of teeth" (Matt. 13 : 42). Tityre also employs a *bineur*; this neologism, derived from *biner,* may refer to a priest who reads mass twice a day, and then again, more likely, to a tiller in the Lord's field that twice ploughs and hoes the Lord's twofold acre, turning over the old ground of the Jews and the Greeks for the new seed.[5] Tityre then finds work for an *arroseur,* an allusion to the sacrament of Baptism, as well as for an *émondeur* who prunes the tree, who sees to its "spiritual circumcision" (Phil. 3 : 3; Col. 2 : 11). At a later stage in the tree's growth, an *astiqueur* and an *épileur* are added to the staff. The former, in his efforts to polish the tree, to give it luster, and to exalt its splendors, may allegorize the Congregation of Propaganda and the Jesuit order (with its motto *ad majorem Dei gloriam,* "For the greater glory of God"). The *épileur,* with his austere depilating mission, may represent both the Reformed

[5] *Bineur* exemplifies the extent to which lexicographers lag behind common usage. The first mention occurs in the *Grand Robert,* t.I, p. 481 (1953). The *Petit Robert* (1970) defines *bineur, bineuse* as "machine destinée aux binages," tracing these words back to 1860. Neither Littré nor Hatzfeld et Darmesteter, nor the *Dict. de l'Ac. Franç.,* 7th ed. (1884), nor even 20th-century editions of *Le Petit Larousse* listed these nouns. Gide, the wealthy landowner of the 1890s, of course, knew the words, and most likely owned the thing they signify.

churches and the Jansenists who, by ironic contrast to the *astiqueur,* show contempt for worldliness, for those "whose adorning [is] that outward adorning of plaiting the hair . . ." (I Peter 3 : 3). Tityre's oak is now given an *échenilleur* to protect it against caterpillars, embodiments of evil. The Serpent is called a worm by Milton in *Paradise Lost.* The caterpillars recall Blake's worm in the rose.[6] Finally, a number of *garçons fruitiers* are employed, no doubt to harvest the fruits of the tree.

In a word, Tityre has left nothing to chance. The offices instituted by him testify to his anxious care for the well-being of his tree. But the strict division of labor in the service of his tree seems to establish differences rather than a common body of communicants that might benefit here and now

[6] "The Sick Rose," from Blake's *Songs of Experience.*

> O Rose, thou art sick!
> The invisible worm
> That flies in the night
> In the howling storm
>
> Has found out thy bed
> Of crimson joy,
> And his dark secret love
> Does thy life destroy.

See also stanzas 3 and 4 of "The Human Abstract" from the same collection.

> He sits down with holy fears
> And waters the ground with tears;
> Then Humility takes its root
> Underneath his foot.
>
> Soon spreads the dismal shade
> Of Mystery over his head;
> And the caterpillar and fly
> Feed on the Mystery.

On the churches as Satan's mills, see Blake's *Milton*:

> And was Jerusalem builded here
> Among these dark Satanic Mills?
> [*Milton,* f. 2]

from the fruit of his oak. The rules governing everyone's functions suggest by the minute details of their provisions that, in the broadest possible sense, Tityre cannot see the forest for his tree. It becomes gradually evident that his sense of duty and order overshadows the very values which his tree allegorizes, that in everything he meticulously observes not the spirit but the letter. His measures intimate a moral lesson; namely that his hierarchic establishment and its demands for the punctilious observance of a complex and rigid ritual appear altogether to inhibit the gratuitous mystical experience of the individual as well as his joyous, free, and liberating participation in the mystic body of the community of communicants. The tree as an organization, imposing itself on the tree as life, reminds one of the churches which have become the "dark Satanic mills" for Blake.

Ménalque's Satanic idea, fully grown with the aid of God owing to the freedom granted to Tityre's will, has driven Tityre from the promise of a golden age into the hell of civilization. In a biblical sense, he has forsaken the tree of life, the spirit, for the tree of knowledge, the law, the letter. In an Arcadian sense, he has neglected his pastoral calling in favor of his political ambitions. The oak's acorns exist for the oak's sake, not as food for the hungry sheep who "look up and are not fed" by their bishop, the Good Shepherd's deputy, whose efforts are now fully devoted to the city he has created, *civitas Dei*, the city of God. Its symbol too is the oak, the sacred tree consecrated to Zeus-Iuppiter, the protector of the polis, the state, Ζεὺς Πολιεύς, Iuppiter Stator (cf. Plutarch *Cor.* 3). Since Tityre's wealth increases at the rate of his oak's growth, he must now employ a number of officers in charge of his riches, of government, and of censorship; he creates the Curia. There is a *comptable*, "pour régler les paiements de chacun" (336); he may be in charge of absolution (with its roots in economic language, "to set free" from debts, etc.), the traffic in indulgences (partial and plenary), and the whole business of keeping track of the believers' credit in the economy of salvation. In his task he is aided by a cashier, who shares with him "le souci de la fortune de Tityre" (336), and whose duties may consist in taking care of the Church's fortunes as well as those of Tityre's reputation as Christ's deputy on earth, infallible in matters of doctrine. Quarrels break out between the *astiqueur* and the *épileur* about the limits imposed on their functions—a dual reference perhaps to the Reformation and to the embittered infighting between Jesuits and Jansenists in the seventeenth century for the privilege of maintaining schools. But it is also an allusion to their doctrinal polarity, the *astiqueur* believing that polishing (transigence, polish, politeness) and the splendors of the baroque (*le style jésuite!*) are fully reconcilable with the Christian life, and the sternly pessimistic *épileur* taking all compromise with worldly adornments for signs of perdition and calling for depilation at the very roots of the evil. Realizing the need for an *arbitre*, Tityre installs such a judge (the Holy Office of the Inquisition, *Sacra Congregatio Romanae et Universalis Inquisitionis seu Sancti Officii*). The *arbitre* is flanked by two lawyers, *pour et contre* (336). His task, too, is ambivalent: in a narrower sense, he seems to represent the *liber arbiter* of the individual, the inner voices which argue *pour et contre*, the *advocatus Dei* that pleads for the good and the *advocatus diaboli*, defending the side of evil. In a wider sense, the *arbitre* maintains the balance between the doctrines of necessity and of the freedom of the will, while, in his inquisitorial role, flanked by his two lawyers, he copes with the problems of heresy and censorship. The inquisitorial court is given a *secrétaire* who files away their judgments (condemnations of heretics as well as *Index librorum prohibitorum*) for future reference with a *garde des arrêts*, no doubt an allusion to the secular arm of the state which executed the judgments of the Inquisition. With the continuous and somewhat chaotic growth of the *civitas Dei*, the Holy Office is given the authority to police the new houses (sects) which spring from the soil: "Du sol cependant les maisons peu à peu s'élevèrent; et il fallut une police des rues, des agents contre leur licence" (336).

Under the burden of his occupations, Tityre falls ill (his salvation is endangered!). He is advised to take a wife. But remaining faithful to the ecclesiastical rule of celibacy, "il fut forcé de se choisir un adjoint ce qui fit qu'on le nomma maire" (336). The *adjoint* now stands for the fully appointed Curia; Tityre's absolute authority as *maire* (Latin, *major*), as "the greatest," as the chief administrator, is now doctrinally asserted. "Dès lors il ne lui resta que trop peu de loisir où pouvoir pêcher à la ligne, des fenêtres de sa maison qui continuaient d'ouvrir continuellement sur les marais" (336). In *Paludes*, too, Tityre was a fisherman (94). Tityre-Petrus, the symbol of the Apostolic Succession, has no time left for his missionary activities; he must neglect his *pêche à la ligne*, his fishing for souls (John 21 : 11), in favor of his administrative duties. The pleonastic repetition *continuaient . . . continuellement* points to a hopeless perpetuation of the morass of human corruption, visible, forever and as far as the eye reaches, from the windows of the Church; a morass going back throughout man's past and stretching into his future with little hope for redemption. Tityre resigns himself to the institution of "jours de fête pour que son peuple pût s'amuser" (336), to saints' days, but amusements, bread and circus, are expensive, and since his subjects are poor he begins to tax them "pour pouvoir leur en prêter à tous" (336); the traffic in indulgences is introduced, in loans which purport to afford some temporary amusement, some time off from Purgatory, to the impoverished sinner whose credit is obviously not good enough to provide him with the blessings of the

eternal joys of Paradise. But "qui fait l'ange, fait la bête":
Tityre's legalistic concerns place his new *civitas* under the
law which by Pauline definition is inimical to grace. The oak
fails to reach up into celestial heights despite the *civitas Dei*
which surrounds it, despite the efforts of its numerous care-
takers: "Or le chêne, au milieu de la plaine (car malgré la
ville, malgré l'effort de tant d'hommes, ce n'avait jamais pu
cesser d'être la plaine), ce chêne, dis-je, au milieu de la plaine,
n'avait aucune peine à être placé de telle sorte que l'un de ses
côtes était à l'ombre, l'autre au soleil" (336). The oak remains with the cities of the plains, its roots deeply sunk in
the human morass, one of its sides exposed to the sun (the
Catholic south), the other side lying in the shade (the Protestant north). Tityre finds the justification of his righteousness
in the shadow of the law, *umbra in lege* (Ambrosius, *In
psalm* 38, n. 25, Migne, *Patrologia Latina*, xiv, 105f.), in the
unenlightened Old Law, in the shade of a joyless Protestantism which banishes the sensual forms of worship, the symbolic lights in churches, the truth shining through pagan
myths—which in short suppresses the external light com-
munally enjoyed. On the sunny side he manures his tree ("du
côté du soleil, il faisait ses besoins naturels," 336), signifying the Catholic tradition's greater readiness to accept the
tributes of the body, as well as its greater awareness of the
common necessities of humanity. Tityre may not deserve
any particular commendation for doing what comes naturally
to him, and yet it has benefited both the tree and the earth,
and given him joy. On the North, he would have died of
constipation.

"Et Tityre était heureux, car il sentait sa vie utile aux autres, excessivement occupée" (336). With his attention divided between the shady and the sunny sides of his tree, it
is hard to tell what Tityre enjoys more, his natural functions
or his practice of the Old Law. Although they keep him ex-

cessively busy, he seems to derive no mean satisfaction from the false values of *negotia,* of his business, of an altruism which for all intents and purposes benefits the tree rather than his community. His feeling of usefulness stems from his devotion to his *idée fixe* and from his attachment to his tree, the dubious gifts of Ménalque to which he enslaves everyone else, while he as piously misinterprets them as he loyally serves them—thanks to the equivocal blessing of the freedom of will given him by the irony of God. It is a precarious free will, predetermined by the acceptance of Ménalque's idea, which appears to cancel out Tityre's freedom of choice.

4. L'Effort de l'homme est cultivable

Like Gide's *Le Retour de l'enfant prodigue* (1907), "Histoire de Tityre" is structured like a triptych. Its first picture ends with the threefold symbol of *arbor crucis,* the tree of the cross. The second picture parodies the institutions and the Reformation of the Church. Here all activity seems to take place in a vacuum, and business appears to be transacted for business' sake, in treadmill fashion, for no one's benefit. Not man but man's effort is cultivable; "l'effort de l'homme est cultivable" (336) is the axiom with which part II of "Histoire de Tityre" begins. It sounds like an abstract variation of Genesis 3 : 19, "In the sweat of thy face shalt thou eat bread," suggesting that nothing has changed since the expulsion of Adam and Eve from Paradise. "L'activité de Tityre, encouragée, semblait s'accroître: son ingéniosité naturelle lui proposant d'autres emplois, on le vit travailler à meubler, tapisser et aménager sa demeure" (336). Not his devotion to the supernatural, not his mystical ecstasy increase, but his "natural ingenuity." It helps him in his attempts to furnish the earthly *demeure,* the resting place of natural man, of the old Adam. His skillfulness is limited to matters of em-

piricism, to the nontheoretical, nonspiritual, and purely literal interpretation of experience as well as to its practical
application, but it is also (in the broadest sense of the word
"ingenuity") confined to a sort of quackery. "Industrieux, il
excellait dans l'empirisme; il inventa même, pour accrocher
ses éponges au mur, une petite patère acrostiche, qu'au bout
de quatre jours il ne trouva plus commode du tout" (337).
The adjective *acrostiche* (see below) which qualifies *patère*
provides a discreet hint to the fact that Tityre's invention
(or discovery) is not primarily a "hat-peg" but rather a pagan
patera, as used at funeral rites in Roman antiquity for sprin-
kling the tomb with bacchantic wine sacrifices. About A.D. 390
Augustine describes such a rite performed over the grave of
Flavius Natalis; his description indicates that this pagan
ceremony was continued in early Christian practices by analogy with the Holy Eucharist. Like the celebration of the Last
Supper (*sub utraque specie*), the wine sprinkled on the grave
of Flavius Natalis announced his redemption, "hic enim
sepulti decumbunt"—*decumbere* being used in its dual meaning of "to rest" and "to banquet." Most likely, as in Old
French usage, *patère* is here assimilated to *patène*. Gide may
have thought in particular of the famous paten among the
French crown treasure, the paten of Saint-Cloud, which is
adorned with eight fishes and was used for the offertory. If
this be so, the adjective *acrostiche* would be brought into
focus: the acrostic ἰχθύς, "fish," accepted by the primitive
Church as a symbol for Christ's name, is said to go back to
a virulent pamphlet of Sybilline origins predicting the fall
of Rome and the resurrection and eternal beatitude of the
just.[7] The eight fishes on the Saint-Cloud paten would also
recall, in this context, Peter's legendary draught of fish, and
the symbolic number for baptism (eight). By extension, the

[7] Cf. E. Renan, *Les Origines du Christianisme* (Paris, 1883), Index
vol., p. 286.

paten would thus evoke the octagonal baptistry and strength-
en the allegorical meaning of *éponge*, the sponge, by which it
signifies the washing away of sin in baptism. Simultaneously,
the sponge, which in the Greek liturgy serves as a purificator
for removing the remnants of the host from the patena, is
meant to recall the sponge filled with vinegar, the drink
given by Elias to Jesus on the cross (Matt. 27 : 48). These
associations modify the image of *patère* (*patène*) *acrostiche*
and the meaning of *empirisme*, punning both on Tityre's
see in the former Roman Empire—in Rome itself, near the
Pontine marshes!—and on the empiric skills of assimilation
for which the Roman Church is famous, and which resulted
in its penetration by pagan rites until deep into the fourth
century of the Christian era (*quatre jours*).[8] Tityre proves his
empiricism quite literally by the institution of a "two chamber" system: "Et Tityre, à côté de sa chambre, fit bâtir une
chambre pour les intérêts de la nation; les deux chambres
avaient même entrée, pour tâcher d'indiquer que les intérêts
étaient les mêmes" (337). Gide's time is cyclical, not linear;
pagan, not Christian; in the seasonal tradition of Greek myth.
Hence, what happened once before happens again in a slightly modified form. Again it is shown how the Church opens
its gates for the Jews (the chamber of Tityre, originally Peter,
the apostolic Jew) and for the Gentiles (the chamber of the
pagans, τὰ ἔθνη, Latin *gens*, *gentiles*, *nationes*, Rom. 9 : 24,
30, etc.). The chamber of the New Testament, predominant-

[8] In the *Prométhée*, time is neither objective nor subjective. It is
dépaysé, mythical, absurd. Time indications vary from suggestions of
month, decade, and hour (without a date) (303) to mention of hour
and season ("entre quatre et cinq heures d'automne," 304). Like the
spiraling and repetitive action it encompasses, time is not linear but
cyclical in this *sotie*, and time units occur on the parabolical level of
actual timelessness. Thus a day may stand for an aeon, or, as we assume
it does here, for a century: the "quatre jours" seem to indicate the
fourth century, during which the Christian Church still absorbed a
variety of pagan rites.

ly open to the heathens, is uncomfortably close to that of the Old Covenant. Both chambers are filled with the same air— a common inspiration—thanks to the one entrance which leads into them. But their neighborhood causes considerable inconveniences to all concerned. When a fire is lit in one chamber, smoke invades the other one; the two chimneys literally cannot draw together. "Mais, à cause de l'entrée commune qui donnait même air aux deux pièces, les deux cheminées ne pouvaient tirer ensemble, et, par les temps froids, quand on faisait feu dans l'une, on faisait de la fumée dans l'autre" (337). When the relationships between the two groups cool off ("par les temps froids"), there are few points of contact left between the ecclesiastical fumes of incense, this vague modification of pagan sacrificial rites, and the Lord of the Jews leading them in a pillar of fire (Exod. 13 : 21; 14 : 24) and appearing to his people in Moses's burning bush and in thunder and lightning on Mount Sinai—and this in spite of the *même air*, the common inspiration of the Bible shared by the Jews and the "nations." "Les jours où il voulait faire du feu, Tityre prit donc l'habitude d'ouvrir sa fenêtre" (337). In order to allow his fervor to rise to heaven, Tityre opens his window, perhaps to see if the Lord of hosts "will not open [unto him] the windows of heaven" (Mal. 3 : 10). As the "catholic" spiritual leader or protector ("Ti-tyre protégeait tout," 337), he works at "la propagation des espèces" (337), but less in a biological sense than in the medi-cal and economic sense of the Christian vocabulary of salva-tion (which would also apply to the financial wealth of the Church), and in the sense of the theological concept of the Species present in the Holy Eucharist. Thus Tityre works toward the propagation of the Church's revenues, its coins (*espèces*), while propagating the economy of salvation and redemption, as well as the spread and sanctification of the

Eucharist in its consecrated Species (*espèces*), the Host and the Wine of the Mass, the Body and the Blood of Christ.

5. Le Tityre mal enchaîné

"Un temps vint que les limaces se promenèrent dans les allées de son jardin en si grande abondance que, de peur d'en écraser une, il ne savait où poser pied, et finit par se résigner à moins sortir" (337). The slimy slugs (*limaces*) which are now teeming in his garden, wallowing in the mud (*limon*), filth, and mire of his swamp (*limus*)—allegories of the clergy emblematically veiled by the Christian equivalent of *limus*, the girdle or apron trimmed with purple, worn by the sacrificing priests in ancient Rome (cf. Virgil *Aen.* 12. 120: *velati limo*)—cause Tityre to withdraw in self-communion, to indulge in some soul-searching. In protest, he now lives in his innermost self; Protestantism begins, the Reformation sets in: "Il fit venir une bibliothèque circulante, avec une loueuse de livres, chez qui il prit un abonnement. Et comme elle s'appelait Angèle, il prit coutume d'aller tous les trois jours passer chez elle ses soirées" (337). Bibliothèque, originally meaning both the locale of a library and a collection of books, is used here in the latter sense, qualified by *circulante* to evoke the dissemination of learning during the Renaissance, the propagation in particular of the Good Book, of *biblía*, the Holy Scriptures, free of apocrypha and in their original version. *Loueuse de livres* is a lending librarian, but beyond that a pun suggesting someone who praises books (*louer*, "to lend" and "to praise"; *loueur, loueuse*, "lender," "praiser")—figuratively speaking, a person who praises the Christian Logos in its mirror-image, the word of the Scriptures. Angèle, ἀγγελία, *annuntiatio*, is the "message" and "annunciation" of the doctrine (I John 1 : 5; 3 : 11); Angèle, the good Angèle, εὐαγγέλιον, *evangel*, the lady friend and abortive muse of the ineffectual writer Tityre in Gide's *Paludes*, now becomes an emblem of the authoritative Scripture, the inseparable companion of Tityre, the *évangélique*, in his transition from Roman Catholicism to the evangelizing activities of the reformer who is almost ready to give up his celibacy. With Angèle he studies "thrice every week" a trinity of disciplines: metaphysics (the study of the last things), algebra (here used in the literal meaning of its Arabic root *al-jabr*, a "reuniting of broken parts," i.e., textual criticism, hermeneutics, attempts to establish the Scriptures in their purity, free from apocrypha), and theodicy (a vindication of God's justice in ordaining or permitting natural and moral evil in the world). These suggestions are given substance by allusions to the iconoclasm of the Reformation. In their cultivation of "différents beaux-arts d'agrément," Tityre accedes to Angèle's "goûts particuliers pour la musique," in conformity with the Protestant trend to further the art of religious music, vocal and instrumental: ". . . ils louèrent un piano à queue, sur lequel Angèle exécutait les petits airs qu'entre temps il composait pour elle" (337). The image of the grand piano, in German *der Flügel* ("wing")—a term doubtlessly familiar to Gide, who read Goethe in the original, and who, as an enthusiast of the piano, played Bach and Beethoven among others—underscores the allegorical significance of Angèle not only as an angelic messenger, but as the very emblem of the Scriptures; it hints at the winged animals which belong to the iconology of the four Evangelists and to that of the Apocalypse. Even the spelling of *entre temps* (instead of the more current *entre-temps*) seems to point to the apocalyptic meaning of these pious, evangelizing "airs": "between" appears here to suggest "between the aeons," between the Incarnation of the Lord and His Second Coming.

Tityre's conversion to Protestantism takes place after a thorough self-examination, in an intimate dialogue with Angèle; his religious and worldly attitudes are henceforth determined by his individual interpretations of scriptural passages. He now recognizes the threat of death which his exclusive cares for his tree constitute for him: "Tant d'occupations me tueront," he complains, "je n'en puis plus; je sens l'usure; ces solidarités activent mes scrupules; s'ils augmentent, je diminue" (337). (Tityre in *Paludes* [126] and Prometheus [327], too, speak in the spirit of John 3 : 30.) He feels not merely weary ("je sens l'usure") of his former preoccupations, which he can no longer tolerate ("je n'en puis plus"), but he also senses the usury (*usure*) involved in the traffic of indulgences and similar practices, which were the pretexts if not the true causes for the reformers' revolt against the ecclesiastical establishment. The use of the present tense, the staccato sentences in rapid sequence, accentuate this climate of revolt. *Solidarité* points to the archaic concept in Roman Law according to which each person in a group was responsible for the totality of a debt contracted together. In other terms, *solidarité* evokes emblematically the community of sinners gathered in the Church, as well as de Maistre's theory of *réversibilité* where the seemingly innocent will pay for the guilty party. The scruples, which diminish Tityre while they augment, are analogous to Prometheus's devouring eagle, and even to the aspect he had offered to the skeptical and contemptuous passersby in Paris, the modern Babel ("tout au plus une conscience," 314). Like Schiller's Zeus, Tityre now asks, "Que faire?" To Angèle's tempting and tentative question, "Si nous partions?" (the open invitation of an evangelist, only to follow the Gospel!) Tityre hesitatingly answers at first, "Je ne peux pas, moi: j'ai mon chêne" (337). The self-assertive "moi" shows his willful attachment to a property which is burdensome and may cause his death, but from which he is seemingly unwilling to separate himself. He still feels hopelessly bound to the Church, to his oak. Angèle insists, "Si vous le laissiez [le chêne]" (337). "Laissez mon chêne! y pensez-vous?" By repeating "mon chêne," Tityre reveals his obsession with the oak, which possesses its owner. It demonstrates his firm belief in the idea which the tree, as an earthly and worldly copy, merely symbolizes. Angèle indirectly but strongly suggests that the oak is no longer a means but an end in itself: "N'est-il pas assez grand bientôt pour pousser seul?" (337). Once more Tityre resignedly shows his attachment to his tree: "Mais c'est que j'y suis attaché." His reply is given in the passive voice of a verb which in itself expresses a passivity, suffering, while identifying by association Tityre's oak with the cross, "nailed to the cross" being rendered in French by "attaché à la croix."

Angèle's nonchalant and utterly feminine command, "Détachez-vous," is all that is needed to persuade Tityre. He now smilingly parts with his oak and his painfully felt solidarity, seeking freedom in his protest. The evangelical Catholic has become a reformer. Like the poorly bound Prometheus, who had left the mountains of Caucasus, Tityre now leaves the hardened soil (Peter's rock) which the roots of his oak had dried out, just as he half audaciously leaves behind almost all the ties which had attached him to his tree. But his detachment is not complete: "Peu de temps après, ayant bien éprouvé que, somme toute, les occupations, responsabilités et divers scrupules, non plus que le chêne, ne le tenaient, Tityre sourit, prit le vent, partit, enlevant la caisse et Angèle et vers la fin du jour descendit avec elle le boulevard qui mène de la Madeleine à l'Opéra" (337f.). He merely flees from one error into another, enacting the *sotie* of an escape without redemption. Even though he follows an inspiration ("il prit le vent") and escapes with Angèle (the pure Gospel), ridding himself of his ritual occupations, responsibilities, and "diverse scruples"—perhaps even of his celibacy (although this point is debatable)—in order to devote himself entirely to the Scriptures, the spirit of the "good message," of ἀγγελία, remains a closed book to him, despite Angèle's physical presence. For though he has given up his tree, he has kept his supposed riches, the cash register, which he carries with him in the erroneous belief that it might contain his salvation, buy his redemption, and prove to be the savings which might save him. Burdened with the Church's wealth, which he has usurped, and accompanied by Angèle, whom he misunderstands, he has failed to comprehend what for Gide is the essential lesson of the Gospels: "If thou wilt be perfect, go and sell that thou hast, and give to the poor, and thou shalt have treasure in heaven: and come and follow me" (Matt. 19 : 21).[9] As a rich man he is excluded from the kingdom of heaven (Matt. 19 : 24). On the Parisian grand boulevard,

---

[9] Once more, Gide's mirror technique is used here with subtle irony. Virgil's Tityrus is granted freedom and savings, moderate wealth, very late in his life. In the presence of Galatea, "nec spes libertatis erat, nec cura peculi" (Ecl. 1. 32). Both are given him in Rome, when he is an old man: "Libertas, quae sera tamen respexit inertem, / candidior postquam tondenti barbi cadebat ("Freedom which, despite my disinterest, came late to me / My beard was clipped whiter now," Ecl. 1. 27). In Rome he beholds the "divine young man for whom our altars smoked every year twice during six days" (Octavian) (Ecl. 1. 42) and who sets him free.

Gide's Tityre, however, flees with Angèle and the peculi (la caisse). Unwillingly he meets the "divine young man" (Moelibée), who in tacit reproach and narcissistically holds out to him tityros, his shepherd's flute.

Gide's mirror technique has dual aspects here: (1) it reflects Tityre's mirror-image by way of the flute metaphor which suggests Tityre's name, and by way of the tityros melody which has preceded the coming of Moelibée; (2) it produces a true mirror-image by reversing the image: not Tityre but Moelibée makes his pilgrimage to Rome, arm in arm with Angèle, while Tityre—abandoned by all—finds himself again where he had started, surrounded by swamps, in a wasteland.

Tityre now finds himself in the very center of historicity and of the modern Babel where, according to I Peter 5 : 13, Christ will appear to the elect.

6. *Apocalypse*

"Ce soir-là l'aspect du boulevard était étrange. On sentait que quelque chose d'insolite, de solennel se préparait. Une foule énorme, sérieuse, anxieuse, se pressait, encombrant le trottoir et débordant presque sur la chaussée qu'à grand-peine maintenaient libre des gardes de Paris échelonnés" (338). The final picture of the Tityre triptych opens with a scene vibrant with apocalyptic expectations. "Devant les restaurants, les terrasses, disproportionnément élargies par le déploiement des chaises et des tables, faisaient l'obstruction plus complète et rendaient la circulation impossible" (338). Since the restaurant, throughout the *Prométhée*, serves as the symbol for a church, one is faced here with an unusually chaotic churchyard scene, disproportionate to the extent of hindering the normal traffic of city life. "Parfois un regardeur impatient se juchait sur sa chaise un instant, le temps qu'on le priât d'en descendre. Evidemment tous attendaient; on sentait à n'en pas douter qu'entre les berges du trottoir, sur la chaussée protégée, allait descendre quelque chose" (338). The scene evokes the opening of the graves and the arising of the saints in Matthew 27 : 52, telescoped with a Gidean *attente* for the Second Coming of Christ. "A grand-peine ayant pu trouver une table, et la louant à très haut prix . . ." (i.e., praising and treasuring it) "Angèle et Tityre s'installèrent devant deux bocks," the scriptural Communion (Angèle's obviously not coinciding with Tityre's, for he takes his *communio sub utraque specie* quite separately, from his own chalice. The *garçon* answers their equally separate questions on what is expected here. "D'où Monsieur revient-il?" he asks, intimating that Tityre had been here before. He continues: "Monsieur ne sait-il pas qu'on attend Moelibée? C'est entre cinq et six qu'il passe . . ." (at the time of the evening meal, the supper!) "et tenez—écoutez: il me semble déjà que l'on entend ses flûtes" (338)—*tityroi*, the flutes of Moelibée, the shepherd. Meliboeus was the good shepherd who had found and brought up Oedipus (Ioann. Antiochus *Fragm.* 8). Meliboeus was the pilgrim expelled from the old universal Empire in Virgil's first *Eclogue*. "Du fond du boulevard un son frêle de chalumeau s'éleva" (338); it rises (*s'éleva*) from far away but also from the depth (*du fond*) of the boulevard. "La foule plus attentive encore palpita. Le son grossit, se rapprocha" (338); the pulse of new life, anxiously awaited, palpitates, beats in the crowd. The approaching crescendo of Moelibée's flute (*tityros*) moves Angèle: "Oh que c'est émouvant! dit Angèle" (338). "Le soleil déclinant envoyait ses rayons d'un bout à l'autre du boulevard. Et, comme issu des splendeurs du couchant, on vit enfin s'avancer Moelibée, précédé du simple son de sa flûte. On ne distinguait bien d'abord que son allure" (338). Moelibée, the good shepherd, approaches, invisible at first, and preceded by the "simple sound of his flute," which is synonymous with *tityros* (i.e., even before his coming, one heard his airs by way of his instrument, Tityre): "A little while, and ye shall not see me: and again, a little while, and ye shall see me, because I go to the Father" (John 16 : 16). Moelibée's coming takes place in an occidental "twilight of the gods" setting ("le soleil déclinant . . . ; comme issu des splendeurs du couchant"). In the *sotie* of errors which is "Histoire de Tityre," Moelibée is on his way to the Father on earth, to *papa*, to the pope in Rome. His approach leaves Angèle literally and metaphorically "spellbound": "Oh! comme il est charmant! dit Angèle" (338). The song of the flute ("son chant de la flûte," *tityros*) comes to a sudden stop when

Moelibée encounters Tityre. Seeing Angèle, Moelibée reveals his true nature, "et chacun s'aperçut qu'il était nu"
(338). Tityre and Moelibée experience a mysterious shock of
recognition; they seem to feel their affinities without clearly
recognizing them. Moelibée's innocent state of nakedness re-
calls that of Adam and Eve before the fall ("And they were
both naked, the man and his wife, and were not ashamed,"
Gen. 2 : 25). Like Adam and Eve after the fall (Gen. 3 : 7),
the sinful crowd is aware of Moelibée's paradisiac and pagan
nudity; he walks about as the very image of Gide's ideal of
dénuement. "Oh! dit Angèle, penchée sur Tityre, qu'il est
beau! que ses reins sont dispos! que ses flûtes sont adorables!"
(339). Her triple praise coincides with her third laudative exclamation about Moelibée, a scarcely veiled allusion to the
Trinity. Admiring his beauty, the strength of his loins, and
his *tityroi,* she openly worships his procreative and creative
potential, his virility. "Tityre était un peu gêné" (339), mind-
ful, no doubt, of the impotence he has inherited from his
predecessor and namesake in *Paludes.* "Demandez-lui donc où
il va, dit Angèle" (339). Questioning Moelibée, "Où allez-
vous?" Tityre repeats Peter's question to Christ before the betrayal, "Domine, quo vadis?" ("Lord, where are you going?"
John 13 : 36), and also Peter's words before his legendary encounter with the Lord on the Via Appia (cf. the apocryphal
Acts of Peter, 30). Just as Peter, on the Via Appia, learned
from the lips of the Lord that he is going to Rome, there to
be crucified anew, Tityre learns from the lips of Moelibée,
"Eo Romam" ("I am going to Rome" 339)—an answer
which permits similarly ominous conclusions, considering
Gide's views on the Roman Catholic Church and on all or-
ganized religion. And just as Peter on the Via Appia spiritu-
ally identifies with his Master and returns to Rome, there to
be crucified in His name, Moelibée (in a ghastly inversion
of this situation) suggests that he, the allegory of the Lord, by

exchanging his role with that of Tityre, will again be nailed to the cross in Rome, which is by now the Holy See. Before the eyes of the utterly confused Angèle, Moelibée, in a sort of literary charade, fully turns into the mirror-image of Tityre (an identification already suggested by the melody played on his *tityroi*). He does so by uttering the same words which in Virgil's first *Eclogue* (20) Tityrus addresses to Meliboeus: "Urbem quam dicunt Romam," "The city they call Rome" (339). "Angèle: Oh! que c'est délicieux, ce qu'il dit! Qu'est-ce que cela veut dire?" Angèle expresses her enthusiasm, though she does not comprehend a word of Moelibée's Latin. Tityre, the former deputy of Christ on earth (Peter, the apostolic succession), but now a fugitive, the thief of the divine money, clearly understands Moelibée's tacit reproach: all roads of Christianity lead to Rome, to the Pauline and Apostolic Church which has over and over again betrayed the Messiah, nailing him again and again to the cross, be it in the name of Catholicism or of the Reformation. He assures his "chère Angèle," "que cela n'est pas si délicieux que ça; cela veut dire tout simplement qu'il va à Rome" (339). Angèle dreamily exclaims, "Rome! Oh! j'aimerais tant voir Rome!"—*evangelion*, the "good word," would so much have liked to reach Rome.

Moelibée once more plays his "primitive mélodie," his messianic song of a golden age to come. "À ces sons, Angèle exaltée se souleva, se leva, s'approcha, et comme Moelibée arrondissait son bras, elle le prit, et tous deux continuant ainsi le boulevard s'éloignèrent, s'éperdirent, disparurent dans le définitif crépuscule" (339). "Exaltée," "se souleva," "se leva," one verbal adjective and two verbs of elevation indicate what happens to Angèle, who takes Moelibée's arm, which is rounded to form a circle, the figure of divine perfection, eternity, and the infinite. Angèle, the angelic servant of the Lord, *evangelion*, the scriptural record of the Incarnate

Word, follows her Master: "And where I am, there shall also my servant be" (John 12 : 26). The scene is a solipsistic reflection of the Incarnate Word in his own message, which alone follows him without betraying him. Leaving behind them the boulevard, the crowd, and Tityre, they move off in a sort of delirium (s'éperdirent, an archaism meaning "they became frantic, lunatic"), a lunacy recalling the salle des nouvelles lunes where Prometheus had given his discourse. In their turn, they are swallowed by a "definitive twilight" of the gods. The définitif crépuscule, their disappearance from the boulevard of sin, their ascension, are as ambiguous as was their coming and passing. They suggest that no one but the Incarnate Word Himself truly loves and understands His Gospels and is, by turns, loved and understood by them, so that both in a narcissistic and angelic union (à la Swedenborg) they must remove themselves from the eyes of the profane who can only defile them. Then again their supernatural union intimates an eschatological meaning, betokening last things and last days: "Yet a little while, and the world seeth me no more; but ye see me: because I live, ye shall live also" (John 14 : 19).

Once more, a sotie within the sotie has mimed the meaninglessness of the Holy Eucharist if the mystery of the divine-human sacrifice remains unintelligible to the communicants, if the sacrament turns into a hollow rite. It is the unconscious betrayal of Christ by his followers, who must be forgiven, "for they know not what they do" (Luke 23 : 34), a betrayal repeated throughout history with every reformation of the Church and its doctrine. It is the sotie of the eternal return of the redeemer's vision and his ever recurring Promethean crucifixion on the rock instantaneously formed and reformed by petrifaction, the petrification of the dogma. In this manner, Christianity must perpetually run through the cycles of spiritual vision, observance of the sacraments, their petrification in the letter of the ritual, and the "definitive twilight" of the gods, which swallows the promise of redemption.

7. The Last Things Shall Be First

"La foule à présent défrénée s'agitait très tumultueuse" (339). Gide's neologism *défrénée*, like *effréné*, is most likely derived from a crossing of φρήν with *frein*. It is associated with the "frantic" disappearance of Moelibée and Angèle. This crowd of Gentiles (who, as Leo Spitzer has shown, adopted the biblical name for the pagans to set themselves apart equally from the Jews and from the Papists), literally becomes a "headless" community, despiritualized (*dé-frénée*), an undisciplined mob (like a riderless horse, deprived of the mind that works through the *frenum, le frein*), when Moelibée, their spiritual head, voluntarily removes himself from the scene, taking with him the very spirit laid down in the Scriptures, Angèle, the "good word." "De toutes parts on entendait questionner:—Qu'a-t-il dit?—Qu'a-t-il fait?—Quelle est cette femme?" (339). The crowd's confusion over Moelibée's words and actions corresponds to that of some of Christ's disciples after his prophecy that soon they shall not see him, and then again they shall see him (John 16 : 16f.): "They said therefore, What is this that he saith, A little while? We cannot tell what he saith" (John 16 : 18). "Et quand, quelques instants après, les gazettes du soir parurent, une féroce curiosité les enleva comme dans un cyclone . . ." (339). The late news, the evening paper is, in a way, "news of the last things," eschatological news to be read before (the last) supper, like anecdotes, i.e., "things unpublished," about Prometheus and his eagle and about Tityre and his oak. Both of these *inédits* are indeed introduced, by analogy with Christ's parables, in the words "[mais] à ce propos une anecdote" (304, 335).

Les gazettes du soir, this "latest news" which arrive at supper time, are devoured with the same "ferocious curiosity" as was the spectacle of Christ's death on the cross by those who witnessed it. Anselm speaks of *curiositas* as being born of self-will (*ex propria voluntate*); it is anarchic, turbulent, and rebellious, as befits Gide's headless multitude. "De curiositate autem [nascuntur] inquietudo, susurratio, detractio et caetera alia" ("moreover, restlessness, mutterings, slander, etc., are born from curiosity").[10] In fact, since it originates in *propria voluntate* ("self-will"), it is of the same family as the other ills derived from pride and disobedience—blindness, loss of order, alienation from grace. Thomas Aquinas, less inclined than Anselm to define *curiositas* as an evil passion, still contrasts it sharply with *studium.* The very opposite of orderly inquiry, the multitude's *curiosité féroce* whirls up into the sky the late eschatological news. "Et l'on apprit soudain que cette femme était Angèle, et que ce Moelibée était quelqu'un de nu qui s'en allait en Italie" (339). [Praedicamus] Christum crucifixum: Iudaeis quidem scandalum, gentibus (literally, "for the crowd") *stultitiam* ("foolishness," a *sotie*) : "Here are we preaching the crucified Christ; to the Jews a stumbling-block, and to the pagans foolishness" (I Cor. 1 : 23). What is (for the Jews) "this scandalous event," is for the multitude a "foolishness," a naked man, wandering arm in arm with a woman, Christ accompanied by his "good message," Angèle, engaged in a perpetual pilgrimage to Rome, to the eternal city, toward the forever unkept promise of a *civitas Dei,* toward the beatific vision of a supernatural *pax romana in aeternam.*

[10] *De similitudinibus,* ch. 36, in J. P. Migne, *Patrologia Latina,* CLIX, col. 617.

"Alors, toute curiosité retombée, la foule s'écoula comme une eau libre, désertant les grands boulevards" (339). Mistaking its nominal faith in Moelibée and Angèle for a true knowledge of their nature, the multitude now deserts the broad way "that leadeth to destruction" (Matt. 7 : 13), in essence retiring from the world and committing the same error of hubris which a decade after the *Prométhée* misleads Alissa,[11] the pathetically false saint of *La Porte étroite* (1909). The abandoned boulevards turn into a desert, emptied of *la foule,* the multitude, *gentibus,* now flowing like a living stream from what would seem to be the *corpus mysticum,* the *communio sanctorum*—the mystical body, the community of Saints—as though fulfilling the word: "He that believeth on me, as the scripture hath said, out of his belly shall flow rivers of living water" (John 7 : 38). But something is wrong, for a discordant note, sounded by the homonym *s'écoula, saecula,* suggests that this particular stream of *eau libre,* far from communicating with the eternal, is free to flow in the secular order of things. One is tempted to believe that it is filling the swamps of original sin which, all of a sudden, again surround Tityre: "Et Tityre se retrouva seul complètement entouré de marais" (339). For Tityre, the cycle is completed. Again he finds himself where he started, as the old Adam, without his oak and without his idea of the oak, stagnating on his marshes and in the depths of an incurable *marasme* (cf. μαραίνω, *marceo* as a biblical trope for

---

[11] The all but bucolic Alissa Bucolin cultivates her sanctity in the northern gloominess of Fongueusemare, a Norman village whose name connotes an unhealthy climate of moldering waters, not unlike Tityre's swamp. In the Mediterranean atmosphere of Aigues-Vives ("Living Water"), she notices with some horror her growing pagan and mythological closeness to nature (not unlike Tityre who eases his nature on the sunny side of his tree): "Je m'étonne, m'effarouche presque de ce qu'ici [à Aigues-Vives] mon sentiment de la nature, si profondément chrétien [à savoir, Calviniste] à Fongueusemare, malgré moi devienne un peu mythologique" (582).

the "wilting away" of a rich man, e.g., "ita est dives in itineribus suis marescet" "[Like grass in the heat of the sun], so will the rich man wilt in his ways," James 1 : 11). Like the multitude, Tityre had heard the good word without actually understanding it: "When anyone heareth the word of the kingdom, and understandeth it not, then cometh the wicked one, and catcheth away that which was sown in his heart. This is he which received seed by the wayside" (Matt. 13 : 19). Tityre had totally misunderstood the seed which he had received by the wayside from Ménalque, and which with the cruel aid of divine irony had grown in his swamp and his heart—just as Zeus's unrecognizable *carte blanche* for redemption had been for Damoclès a mystifying messenger of death. Both Tityre and Damoclès had failed, for although they had heard the divine word and had even tried to heed it, they had not been granted the grace to understand its meaning. In a Pauline sense they had sinned by meticulously observing the law; they had done so in good faith, but also without faith in the spirit that saves from the letter of the law. In Paul's words: "I cannot understand my own behavior. I fail to carry out the things I want to do, and I find myself doing the very things I hate" (Rom. 7 : 15). In their shortsightedness, their literal-minded willfulness, they could not understand the mysterious and mystifying paradox of the cross: the tree of life concealed in the tree of death, the spirit of life abolishing the letter of the law.

"Mettons que je n'ai rien dit" (339). With these words, Prometheus had prefaced his anecdote (335), and with these words he ends it (339). His conclusion, anticipated before his tale and repeated after it, implies audience participation in the *sotie*. Prometheus's audience is as much of a mirror held up to Damoclès and Tityre as the latter are mirrors held up to Prometheus and his audience. Prometheus's final words imply that his audience (like Damoclès, Tityre, and the multitude in "Histoire de Tityre") will ultimately lack the grace needed for understanding the sardonic lesson of Prometheus's anecdote, just as they had previously failed to seize the meaning of his discourse in the *salle des nouvelles lunes*. Both stories have been blind mirrors in which the audience could not recognize itself. They have been like tales told by an idiot, signifying nothing to an ignorant multitude full of *curiosité féroce* but lacking *studium*, zeal in a Thomist sense. They might as well have been left untold.[12]

[12] For a possible link between "Histoire de Tityre" and Paul Valéry's *Dialogue de l'Arbre*, see my contribution to *Interpretation und Vergleich. Festschrift für Walter Pabst* (Berlin, 1972): "Zu P. Valéry's *Dialogue de l'Arbre*: Das Gedicht von den Antipoden Valéry und Gide."

Four. MORAL: THE LIBERATING LEAP BEYOND HISTORY

1. *Prometheus's Moral: The Eagle as* Nourriture terrestre

"UN RIRE irrépressible secoua quelques instants l'auditoire" (339). The audience reaction seems to justify what foresight (Prometheus) had to foretell: the audience indeed shows no understanding whatever for Prometheus's parable. The irrepressible laughter which greets the (foregone) conclusion of "Histoire de Tityre" confirms that both its form and its lesson (on *Christum crucifixum*) is *gentibus stultitiam* (I Cor. 1 : 23), for the ignorant multitude—a foolishness, *une sottise, une sotie*. Literal-minded and iconoclastic, the multitude fails to perceive the figurative meaning, the spirit behind the letter; it cannot see the satire for the farce. "Messieurs, je suis heureux que mon histoire vous divertisse, dit en riant également Prométhée" (339). The possessive "mon," qualifying "histoire," strongly suggests the identity of his own bondage to the eagle (before he killed it) and Tityre's attachment to his oak. *Divertir* goes back in this context to its primitive strong meaning as an antonym to *convertir*. Prometheus laughs at the paradox of a pharisaic audience, too sophisticated not to laugh at his anecdote and not sophisticated enough to see its serious significance; an audience which is diverted by a parable meant for their conversion, and diverted also by the false doctrines emanating from the history of Prometheus's eagle, mirrored once more in the story of Tityre's oak. It is far from suspecting the historical missions of Prometheus's eagle and Tityre's oak, their literal, i.e., worldly, secular interpretations. Its false beliefs, in fact, are

126

founded upon history itself, on the morbid hope of better things to come, just as Prometheus had said in his discourse in the *salle des nouvelles lunes*: "Non plus croyance au bien, mais malade espérance du mieux. La croyance au progrès, Messieurs, c'était leur aigle" (324). With the failing belief "au bien," in the true wealth of redemption, *et nunc*, now, with the naïve faith in progress revealing itself in the history of civilization and the Church begins Christianity's eagle: the eschatology of an *histoire universelle* which for Bossuet would lead from Adam's fall via Christ's death on the cross to the Last Judgment, and in the modern layman's breviary of the proletariat to the paradise of classless society. Regardless of whether it is oriented toward a supernatural beyond or toward a golden age in this world, this ill-fated hope for better things to come is the aerie in which is hatched the eagle's egg of faith in the supernatural powers of history to lead man to his future redemption. For Gide, as later for Albert Camus, his spiritual son, *ferveur* and *attente* are mystical states of readiness for communion and communication here and now. The denigration of the present is superstition, heresy, false prophecy, metamorphosing the here and now into a gloomy state of transition, depriving it of the eternal joys of life, and cheating fate by stripping it of its dignity and its tragic meaning. It denies the essence of life in a manner analogous to that of the eagle in devouring Prometheus's vital substance, of Damoclès's scruples in destroying his existence, and of Tityre's oak in reducing to naught his joie de vivre. It constitutes self-flagellation, mortification of the flesh, the renunciation of life itself by believers who are deluded by their faith in benefits to come after death. These seeming gains, derived from misunderstood loans out of the coffer of grace, belong to a divine "Miglionnaire"-banker, who for his own amusement ties down his creatures with illusory wealth, while simultaneously exacting the repudiation of all ties and property.

The weak fetters which bind Prometheus to the rock of history prove not to be morally binding. They reveal themselves as historical self-knowledge and consciousness of guilt, as conscience destroying beauty and innocence, as the historical superstition of progress (either in its original Christian doctrinary form, or in the Hegelian and Marxist modifications of Christian doctrine). As such they belong in the pantheon and mausoleum of dead values, where those who are dead to the joys of the present bury their dead with false hopes of a utopian future. In a Freudian sense (before Freud), the meaning of Prometheus's ironic laughter and the contemptuous *rire irrépressible* of his audience ambiguously contains its very opposite. "Depuis la mort de Damoclès, j'ai trouvé le secret du rire" (339f.), admits Prometheus in a confession which is obviously a false one, for as Foresight incarnate he must have known this secret from the beginning of time. In the new light emanating from his anecdote, the secret of laughter consists in the participation, *et nunc*, at the banquet of life, the Holy Eucharist. "A présent j'ai fini, Messieurs," (to be added: "avec mon aigle, mon histoire"), "laissons les morts ensevelir les morts et allons vite déjeuner" (340). As though to illustrate that here, at last, begins the true institution of the Eucharist, the end of the long fast and of death's reign, Prometheus leaves the cemetery of history, arm in arm with the *garçon* and Coclès, in the company of the irrepressibly laughing audience. "Il prit le garçon par le bras, Coclès par l'autre; tous sortirent du cimetière" (340). Once outside the graveyard gates, the multitude again scatters.

Coclès and the *garçon* now remain alone with Prometheus. In a confused sort of prayer, Coclès now asks Prometheus for forgiveness ("Pardonnez-moi" 340), and declares himself spellbound by "Histoire de Tityre" ("votre récit était charmant," 340), and diverted by it ("vous nous avez bien di-

verti," 340), turned away perhaps from his fruitless quest
for another divine slap in the face. But he fails to see the
point, ". . . mais je ne saisis pas le rapport. . . ." Before he
can finish, Prometheus interrupts him with a fideistic hint,
suggesting Coclès ought to abstain from attempting to comprehend by way of reason the impenetrable mystery: ". . . ne
cherchez pas à tout cela trop grand sens; je voulais surtout
vous distraire, et suis heureux d'y être parvenu; vous devais-je
cela? Je vous avais tant ennuyés l'autre fois" (340). The boredom caused "the other time" by Prometheus's discourse in
the *salle des nouvelles lunes*, by inviting everyone to feed
the eagle, symbol of his secular ills, with his own flesh, had
had the diabolical overtones of Baudelaire's ennui, of the
troubles grown out of Ménalque's seeds, and of Chateaubriand's *mal du siècle*. It had given Damoclès those chills
which had finally led to his death. Prometheus's anecdote of
Tityre and his tree was intended to pay a questionable debt
to the audience, and to make up for the morbid and mortal
consequences of his previous discourse, by distracting his
listeners from their ennui, from their secular bondage. "The
hour will come—in fact it is here already [*et nunc est*]—when
the dead will hear the voice of the Son of God, and all who
hear it will live" (John 5 : 25). With Prometheus, Coclès
and the *garçon* are now allowed to enter the new aeon of
eternal life here and now, the era of the efficient Eucharist
(John 4 : 14; 6 : 51; 8 : 51; 11 : 26, etc.). "Où allons-nous?
dit le garçon," indicating his humble willingness, after their
return to the boulevards, to follow Prometheus wherever he
may lead him, to the broad ways of sin in the world of the
living. "A votre restaurant, si vous le voulez bien, en souvenir
de notre première rencontre" (340). The celebration in memory of the Last Supper will be instituted in the café,[1] which

---

[1] A return to the early Christian commemoration of the Last Supper,
κοινωνία, which was not formal. Early Christians commemorated the

had been the scene of Prometheus's first meeting with Coclès, Damoclès, and the *garçon*, as well as of the abortive descent of the Holy Ghost. "Vous le passez," says the *garçon* to Prometheus, who did not recognize it, because (as he now remarks) its window front is totally changed. "C'est qu'elle est toute neuve [la devanture], à présent" (340), replies the *garçon*, hinting at reforms going far beyond those instituted by the Reformation: an abolition of the Pauline *attente* for life after death, a readiness for the new life *à présent, et nunc*. Prometheus now remembers that his eagle had destroyed the café's large picture window, through which those within could safely look at the broad way of sin, while those without, the passersby, were able to catch fleeting glances of representations of Communion in the Holy Trinity (*des tables de trois*, 305). "J'oubliais que mon aigle. . . . Soyez tranquilles: il ne recommencera plus" (340), he says—an ambiguous anacoluthon, for it implies on the one hand that the eagle will never break windows again, never again descend tempestuously as an iconoclastic spirit of reforms which bring about no essential changes, and on the other hand that the Holy Spirit may never be poured out again. But he will never have to descend again, for now he is going to be eaten ("nous allons le manger," 340), and will become here and now an integral part of the living community. The joyous banquet of Coclès and the *garçon* in the true presence of Prometheus (and upon his instant invitation) accomplishes the miracle of Holy Communion in the spirit by the reception of the spirit in their "hearts" (Gal. 4 : 6) (for the ancients as well as in colloquial French interchangeable with "stomachs," e.g.,

---

Last Supper with the love feast of agape, whose excesses Paul criticized in these words: "So then when you meet together, it is no longer possible to eat the Lord's Supper. For at the meal, each one takes first his own supper, and one is hungry, and another drinks overmuch. Have you not houses for your eating and drinking?" (I Cor. 11 : 20-22) *mal au coeur*). Coclès, the *garçon*, and Prometheus, heartily feasting on the killed eagle, consuming the Holy Ghost together with its mockery (the consciousness of evil, bad conscience), form the only *corpus mysticum* conceivable to Gide: that of communicants who here and now experience the living presence of the Lord, who attain—as Gide put it decades later—"[dès à présent] à la participation immédiate, à la vie éternelle" (Dostoïevsky, 207). The true Eucharist is no longer a rite performed under the guidance of a minister, with the exclusion of the dead and the supposedly damned: the *garçon* is invited to lay down his ministry, the Holy Communion accepts the dead Damoclès in the *coitus sanctorum*, in the intercourse of the Saints. "A *table*," the *garçon* invites, "*Allons! à table, Messieurs!*" (340). But Prometheus commands: "Garçon . . . ne servez pas: en dernier souvenir de lui, prenez la place de Damocle" (340). Damoclès, called lovingly "Damocle," at long last resurrected after his own passion, now becomes an integral part of the Body and Spirit of Christ, in the commemoration of whose Passion the Holy Communion takes place. Here is no sadness, no starvation such as had been visited upon Prometheus during the days of his eagle: "De son temps [de l'aigle] est-ce que j'osais rire? N'étais-je pas maigre affreusement?" Prometheus asks, evoking the anguish and fear of death (*les affres de la mort*) which prevailed during his eagle's lifetime. His words confirm that redemption takes place *à présent*, in a revolutionary reinterpretation of "Blessed are ye that hunger now: for ye shall be filled. Blessed are ye that weep now: for ye shall laugh" (Luke 6 : 21). "Le repas fut plus gai qu'il n'est permis ici de le redire, et l'aigle fut trouvé délicieux" (340). Coclès now asks whether the eagle had been no use at all, to which Prometheus answers: "Ne dites donc pas cela, Coclès! Sa chair nous a nourri. Quand je l'interrogeais, il ne répondait rien" (340f.). Prometheus's reply is disquieting rather than reassuring, for he asserts that while the eagle's spirit yielded no answer, they had derived satisfactory nourishment from its letter ("sa chair nous a nourri"). He continues: "Mais je le mange sans rancune: s'il m'eût fait moins souffrir il eût été moins gras; moins gras il eût été moins délectable" (341). The time of suffering, of weeping and hungering, had had its advantages too (cf. above, Luke 6 : 21). It is implied that the worship of the letter had produced a literature from which Prometheus had suffered, to be sure, but not without some gain for himself—a literature which had also embellished the letter, making it more *délectable*. To Coclès's question, "De sa beauté d'hier que reste-t-il?" Prometheus replies, "J'en ai gardé toutes les plumes" (341), ambiguously suggesting that he alone is the custodian of its former beauty but also the keeper of the quills with which past, present, and future writers recorded and will again record gratuitous accounts of Prometheus and his eagle.

2. Gide's Moral: Aesthetic Disposal of the Eagle of History

The author now intrudes upon his work, confessing that he has written his little book with one of these quills from the plumage of Prometheus's eagle (which is that of an outdated but still venerable Holy Spirit, now fully consumed by Christ's body).[2] It would seem that he was only able to do

---

[2] Gide's ambiguity even prevails in the symbolism of *la plume de l'aigle*, which evokes the wings of the Holy Ghost as well as Victor Hugo's *La Plume de Satan*, redeeming Satan (*La Fin de Satan*), and another feather of Hugo's, angelic this time, in *Les Contemplations* (book 4, *Au Bord de l'infini*, "Les Mages," 5, stanza 3):

> Quelquefois une plume tombe
> De l'aile où l'ange se berçait;
> Retourne-t-elle dans la tombe?
> Que devient-elle? On ne le sait.

this because he thought the quill had been sent him by Prometheus as an *acte gratuit*, like Zeus's initial one bringing into being the *Prométhée*, which is created once more by the *action gratuite* of André Gide (implying that his own hand was guided by Providence-Prometheus) for the benefit (or destruction) of some future *rare ami* Damoclès: "C'est avec l'une d'elles [plumes] que j'écris ce petit livre; puissiez-vous, rare ami, ne pas le trouver trop mauvais" (341).

Prometheus reestablishes moral and morale. Both are resurrected after the interregnum of a "personal" and hence denied morality (*la moralité privée*). The *déjeuner*, the fast broken in honor of Damoclès, the successful reenactment of the Last Supper, a joyful and sacrificial banquet, *et nunc*, represents a spiritual renewal in the flesh in memory of the vanquished fear and threat of death. What is being consumed with the eagle is the Thanatos touch of history and its concept of progress, in the spirit of Nietzsche's vitalistic criticism of history. About his shock of recognition when reading Nietzsche, Gide wrote in 1898: "Je suis entré dans Nietzsche malgré moi; je l'attendais avant de le connaître—de le connaître fût-ce de nom" (*Billet à Angèle*, December 10, 1898, *M.ch.*, 179). He had read Nietzsche in Henri Albert's translation, and he had seen in him the end product of Protestantism, "la plus grande libération" (*M.ch.*, 176). In his discourse, Gide's Prometheus had clearly defined mankind's devouring eagles, by identifying them with human history: "L'histoire de l'homme, c'est l'histoire des aigles,

---

Se mêle-t-elle à notre fange?
Et qu'a donc crié cet archange?
A-t-il dit non? a-t-il dit oui?
Et la foule cherche, accourrue,
En bas la plume disparue,
En haut l'archange évanoui!

Messieurs" (324). Man's historicity is his loss of innocence.
With his entrance in history, in time, coincides his *conscience d'être*, his search for *raisons d'être*, or (in the terms
of the *garçon*, in the beginning of the *Prométhée*) his quest
for an idiosyncrasy. His belief in history runs parallel to his
faith in progress, both superstitions preventing him from ever
fully living in the present moment (324). His existence is
perpetually threatened with drowning in hopes of a future
utopia, in the stream of promises of "becoming." For Gide,
the liberating qualities of Christianity do not essentially differ from those of pagan Arcadia, sung by Theocritus and
Virgil. His Prometheus almost echoes Baudelaire's "J'aime
le souvenir de ces époques nues."[3] He nostalgically recollects
his impressions of man before he gained consciousness of
his eagle, his *conscience d'être*: "La première conscience qu'ils
eurent [les hommes], ce fut celle de leur beauté. . . . L'homme
se prolongea dans sa postérité" (324). Their unchanging
beauty, repeated from generation to generation, the absence
of differences, constituted their principle of unity, harmony,
communion in a sense of timelessness: "La beauté des pre-
miers se redit, égale, indifférente, et sans histoire" (324).
With history begins ugliness, Hesiod's bad Eris (the daughter
of Night), differences, corruption, but also—for Gide as for
Baudelaire—the attraction and repulsion of a sickly beauty
caused by man's estrangement from nature:

> Nous avons, il est vrai, nations corrompues,
> Aux peuples anciens des beautés inconnues:
> Des visages rongés par les chancres du coeur
> Et comme qui dirait des beautés de langueur. . . .[4]

Christianity lost its potential Arcadian dimension with its
entrance into history, with the Acts of the Apostles, with

[3] *Les Fleurs du mal,* "Spleen et idéal," v.
[4] *Ibid.*

its growing care for order, tradition, rootedness, property, rigid institutions, the family. Petrified in history, beginning with Peter and the Apostolic Succession, it has become divorced from the eternal cycles and seasons of life, and waxed linear, temporal, secular, while hypocritically denouncing the worldly order of things in which it has buried its rich, strong, yet temporal roots like Tityre's tree. On a small scale, Gide's rejection of historical Christianity is illustrated by the clinical histories of Prometheus and his eagle, Damoclès and his death from unmerited and insufficient grace, Tityre and his lack of understanding for Ménalque's dubious gifts. On a larger scale, these parables within parables within parables are variations for Gide on one and the same *sotie*, a nonsensical distortion of Christ's teachings, presented by theologians and philosophers throughout the centuries: the history of mankind as a history leading in a straight line from Adam's fall and God's *gemina praedestinatio* ("twin predestination") to a utopian beyond. Basing themselves on this conception are all Hegelian ideologies of a "world history" (reduced by Nietzsche to the more modest proportions of "human history") as a history of social and economic salvation for the good and doom for the wicked. On this level of interpretation the eagle represents the willfulness of history, whose determinism devours the freedom of the individual to follow his unpredictable drives, to create through his *actes gratuits* a fate wholly his own.

In the *Prométhée*, the universal morality of the acceptance of life here and now is restored, after the events recorded in "Chronique de la moralité privée," after "La Détention de Prométhée," after "Les Derniers Jours et les funérailles de Damoclès." This restoration occurs in the course of "Histoire de Tityre," which results in an irrepressible laughter founded, it is true, on a basic lack of understanding for the mystery recounted, but a laughter liberating all the same, a laughter providing relief for those present. It leads, not for all but for a happy few, to the mystical experience of a joyful Communion and communication in the full renunciation of all attempts rationally to violate a mystifying mystery which is accepted in its inviolability. The moral restoration takes place after the historical events which had led to the death of both Damoclès and Prometheus's eagle and to their burial respectively in the cemetery and in that grotesque allegory of Christ's Body, the community formed by Prometheus, the *garçon*, and Coclès, to which Damoclès is posthumously re-admitted.

When all is said and done, the restored morality of the *Prométhée* commands that the eagle—regardless of the form in which he may appear, be it as a force of history or as the Holy Ghost—must first be cultivated, must feed on those whose lot he is. But in the end, he must be eaten by those whom he has devoured. He must be assimilated in order to be prevented from devouring vital substance. Only in this way, assimilated and transposed, can he again take flight on the wings of an artistic creation, embellished by "one of his own quills" (*plumes*), and assume new forms of life, multivalent and indestructible: not by submitting to the writer's (the communicant's) willfulness, but by the free choice of the road to follow, by an inspired, unpredictable and fateful *acte gratuit*.

3. The Epilogue and Its Moral

If this be the moral and aesthetic lesson of the *Prométhée*, it provides a clue to the "Epilogue pour tâcher de faire croire au lecteur que si ce livre est tel ce n'est pas la faute de l'auteur" (341). It would also explain the motto of the epilogue, an inaccurate quotation from the *Journal des Goncourt*: "On n'écrit pas les livres qu'on veut" (341). Better than that, a close look at the original text, which is reduced here to telegraphic brevity, would confirm our interpretation of the *Prométhée* as primarily a *sotie* of clerical significance: "Toujours la fatalité du livre. Nous dont les sympathies de race et de peau penchent pour le pape, nous qui ne détestons pas l'homme qu'est le prêtre, nous voici à écrire, poussés par je ne sais quelle force irrésistible qui est dans l'air, un livre méchant à l'Église. Pourquoi! Mais sait-on le pourquoi de ce qu'on écrit!"[5] The Goncourt's *captatio benevolentiae*, probably meant to capture the reader's indulgence for *Madame Gervaisais*, could literally be applied to Gide's *Prométhée*, justifying both our moral and aesthetic explication of this work.

In the Epilogue, Pasiphaë speaks Prometheus's language when she defends before her husband her strange interlude with the bull, who here becomes analogous to Prometheus's eagle and Tityre's oak: "Que veux-tu? Moi, je n'aime pas les hommes" (341). She had entered her affair with the bull in the hope "qu'un dieu s'y cachait" (341), an allusion on Gide's part to Phaedra's words to Hippolytos in Ovid's Heroïdes:

> Jupiter Europen (prima est ea gentis origo)
> Dilexit, tauro dissimulante Deum,
> Pasiphae mater decepto subdita tauro
> Enixa est utero crimen onusque suo.
>
> (*Heroïdes*, 4. 55ff.)

> (Jupiter loved Europa—such is the origin of my [Phaedra's] family—the bull concealing the God. Pasiphaë, my mother [hidden in a wooden cow], submitting to the deceived bull, produced from her womb her conviction and her burden [the Minotaur]).

---

[5] *Journal des Goncourt* (Paris, 1888), III, 206. I owe this reference to my friend and colleague, Walter Pabst, of the Freie Universität Berlin.

Gide's Pasiphaë is vexed that her efforts ("et ça n'a pas été facile!") were in vain, for "si Zeus s'en fût mêlé, j'eusse accouché d'un Dioscure; grâce à cet animal je n'ai mis au monde qu'un veau" (341). Her attempt to attract the grace of a *Deus absconditus* had been her temptation, born of hopes which were founded on piety, zeal and the lessons of history. But no *action gratuite* can compel the *Dieu caché* either to reveal his identity (as proven by Damoclès's experience) or to appear on the scene when desired (as proven by Coclès's inability to encounter Zeus again for the purpose of obtaining another slap in the face to benefit his neighbor). Whether it be vivifying or sterile, the divine *acte gratuit* always comes veiled in mystery, as a mystification, exacting a sacrifice. And so does the gratuitous act of artistic creation, using or abusing the artist as its tool, and transforming him in the process. The presence of the unknown God (or book) is concealed under the least suspected animal guise. Grace may at best fall into one's lap (witness Gide's *le Prométhée mal enchaîné*, and, on a considerably more carnal level, the God concealed in Leda's swan and Europe's bull). Or it may destroy one's vision, as literally happens to Coclès in one of his eyes, and figuratively to Damoclès in both. In whatever form *l'acte gratuit* may occur, it hides in its letter an impenetrable blessing or curse. In the light of the spirit, *sub specie aeternitatis*, it may reveal, both for divine and artistic creation, an ironic reversal of essentially ambivalent rewards.

Bibliography

Le Prométhée mal enchaîné was first published in *L'Ermitage*, in January, February, and March 1899. In November 1897, Gide had written to E—— R——: "Je continue à lire Les Déracinés. Ces gens-là [Barrès, Maurras—a homonym for English "morass," French *marais*, and possibly (but not probably) an indirect allusion to Tityre's swamps] me suppriment. . . . Je cherche sous quelle formule religieuse ou morale je peux abriter mon opposition. Je trouve celle de Prométhée: "Se dévouer à son aigle; . . . et suffit!" (1502) This passage seems to confirm my hypothesis, expressed toward the end of the first section of my chapter "Histoire de Tityre," that on the literary level of interpretation the "Histoire de Tityre" is meant—in part at least—to be a satire on Barrès's thesis of uprootedness, with strong hints at Christ's nomadic existence.

Selected Secondary Literature

Albérès, R. M. [pseud. for Marill, R.]. *L'Odyssée d'André Gide*. Paris, 1951 (*Prométhée*, 111ff.).

Brée, Germaine. *André Gide: L'insaisissable Protée*. Paris, 1953 (*Prométhée*, 104ff.).

Holdheim, William W. *Theory and Practice of the Novel: A Study on André Gide*. Geneva, 1968 (*Prométhée*, 190ff.).

Ireland, G. W. *André Gide: A Study of his Creative Writings*. Oxford, 1970 (*Prométhée*, 249-270).

March, Harold. *Gide and the Hound of Heaven*. Philadelphia and London, 1952 (*Prométhée*, 108ff.).

Marchand, Max. *Le Complexe pédagogique et didactique d'André Gide.* Oran, 1954 (*Prométhée,* 47, 174).

O'Brien, Justin. *André Gide: A Critical Biography.* New York, 1953 (*Prométhée,* 15off.).

Painter, George A. *André Gide: A Critical and Biographical Study.* New York, 1957 (*Prométhée,* 57ff.); 2nd ed., 1968 (*Prométhée,* 36ff.).

Pizzorusso, Arnaldo. "*Le Prométhée mal enchaîné* et 'le secret du rire,' " *Revue d'histoire littéraire de la France* (April-June 1966), 283ff.

Savage, Catherine H. *André Gide: L'Evolution de sa pensée religieuse.* Paris, 1962 ("Zeus et Prométhée," 193ff.).

Schildt, Göran. *Gide et l'homme.* Paris, 1949 (*Prométhée,* 55ff.).

Trousson, Raymond. *Le Thème de Prométhée dans la littérature européenne.* 2 vols. Geneva, 1962 (*Prométhée,* 435ff., *passim*).

Watson-Williams, Helen. *André Gide and the Greek Myth.* Oxford, 1967 (*Prométhée, passim*).

Index

PRINCETON ESSAYS IN EUROPEAN
AND COMPARATIVE LITERATURE